Moscow Excursion
by Pamela Lyndon Travers

Address:
HardPress
8345 NW 66TH ST #2561
MIAMI FL 33166-2626
USA
Email: info@hardpress.net

MOSCOW
EXCURSION

by P. L. TRAV

Russia

MOSCOW EXCURSION

MOSCOW EXCURSION

by

P. L. TRAVERS

REYNAL & HITCHCOCK
New York

To
H. L. G.

PREFACE

I wonder if all tourists in their secret hearts feel themselves diddled. Does he who sees the Night Life of Paris from a char-à-banc privately feel, when he returns to his hotel, that his fifty francs might have been better spent; and he who goes on a Round-the-World trip wonder sometimes if he has really seen the world? There can, of course, be no true answer to this question, for when a tourist feels it to be imminent he staves it off by displaying his collection of picture postcards and samples of Benares ware. The tourist returned from Soviet Russia, however, has less tangible but far more subtle trophies. He may not be able to hang up assegais and tiger-skins, but he can dazzle those who listen to his traveller's tale with propaganda and statistics which suggest that since the days of the Old Testament the land of Canaan has moved its domicile considerably to the North-West.

It must be such stories as these that encourage those who have not been to Soviet Russia to believe, and to spread abroad that belief as an axiom, that the tourist is shown only the best of everything. I went to Russia happily infected with this assurance (though I knew that the last thing those who repeated it meant was to be reassuring), and it was with some disappointment that I discovered the statement to be entirely untrue. The real Russia (which for anybody not hopelessly romantic must be the *best* Russia) is as carefully concealed from the vulgar eye of the tourist as were the contents of the sacred Ark from the ordinary Israelite. For him the Ten Days have no reverberations. He knows that they shook the world, but never does their dying thunder impinge upon his ears. It is not allowed to. Instead, Russia Reborn is spread out before him, with its factories, its crèches, its museums, its power-stations—and, indeed, only the outer husks, the thrown skins of these. If technical schools, day-nurseries and electrification plants are all the prospective traveller to Russia wants to see, there is no need for him to spend more money than will buy a ticket to Tunbridge Wells or Brighton. One can almost as easily judge of the external results of the Ten Days by these as by seeing their equivalents in the Soviet State. After all, a Russian baby in a Russian cradle is much the same as a baby in a cradle anywhere else; boot factories and electric-cable pylons all over the world have most points in common.

I suppose it is inevitable that the tourist should be shown such things. He is a pitiable and gullible creature at best. He has no palate and will swallow a boot factory or the British Museum with equal gusto. Besides, the fact that a new country is organized for tourist traffic is sufficient indication that it has settled down and, in following its own pursuits, has no time to indulge the over-curious traveller, though for financial reasons it may encourage his incursions. No. Properly to see Russia one must not be a tourist. One must know the language, move about alone and dispense with the questionable blessing of State guides. With these the traveller with any sense of history finds himself often at variance, for few historical events are recognizable once they have been doctored with Marxism and Expediency. The truth about the past, particularly that part of it that pertains to Tsarism, is so horrible that it really needs no addition. But the guides, whether instructed to do so or because their imaginations are so vivid, are apt to disguise it with Soviet principles, and the poor tourist, courteously ready to see Red in reason, sees too much of it and a *contretemps* occurs. It is this determined falsification more than anything else that makes one react, perhaps too vigorously, against the present Soviet régime. This and the all too evident fact that the new State wrested so nobly and with such heroism from chaos during the Ten Days has developed merely into a new and more vigorous form of bourgeois bureaucracy. Looking for the New one is brought up rudely against the Old—garnished and prinked out in a new hat, of course, but recognizably the old.

The letters that comprise this book record the

9

impressions of one tourist during a recent autumnal tour of the U.S.S.R. They are admittedly entirely personal and prejudiced and were written originally for a single recipient rather than for publication. The title itself will serve as an indication of their purely temporal quality, and anybody who looks to them for a serious exposition of the Soviet State is doomed to disappointment. Contrary to the convention laid down (by precedent if not by law) for writers of books about Russia these letters do not pretend to give the Whole Truth. Neither have they a political bias towards any party. In a world rocking madly between Fascism and Communism the writer prefers the latter form of tyranny if the choice must be made. But it is a desolate alternative, for Communism in Russia is for one class of the community only and thus is hardly on bowing terms with Communism as defined in the dictionaries. But it is only on paper that there exist Communist States where the lion lies down with the lamb, the *kulak* with the proletarian. To suggest that making bedfellows of such opposing forces would bring about the desired Classless Society would be to proclaim one's self lamentably idealistic and humanitarian to the modern Russian whose aim is a mechanized rather than a humanized State.

It is a constant source of surprise to the tourist in Russia that in a country whose goal is admittedly that very Classless Society there should exist

10

so many arbitrary grades and classes. These function within the mould of the State. Outside it, we are led to believe, stalks with the venom and vigor of St. George's Dragon, that bogy-man of modern Russia, the Class Enemy. Decrease as he may in numbers, his shadow does not grow less, for it lies upon every Soviet worker and spurs him on to bigger and better flights of industry. The Class Enemy appears to be a rationalized form of the legendary beasts of old; and that he makes no appearance in these letters is due to the fact that the tourist knows of him only by hearsay, much as the Minotaur was known to the people of Crete. I am sorry to have missed him. All jam and no pill may pall eventually upon the most earnest sybarite.

One can have nothing but admiration for the courage and endurance of a nation bent upon reducing life to its material elements. But while one admires the qualities one need not be pledged to the end to which they move. Belief in the individual and the enlarging of human capacities rather than their curtailment precludes entirely any belief in a Mechanized State, no matter how well planned. Rationalization, carried to its logical conclusion, can mean nothing but death. By breaking a thing up into its component parts we do not find its whole; a dissected body tells us nothing of the life that gave it breath.

But no traveller, certainly no tourist, would

dare to deny that the Russian race, dark, un-known, potential, has within it the power to fuse those elements into an eternal pattern.

It is perhaps necessary to stress the fact that the characters in the book are all synthesized person-ages and that I have studiously given fictitious initials for names throughout. So that should any one, slipping among the paragraphs, imagine that he has come face to face with himself, I take this opportunity of courteously assuring him that he is mistaken. It is *always* some one else.

Extracts from these Letters have appeared in recent numbers of *The New English Weekly* and I am indebted to the Editor for permission to reprint them.

P. T.

March, 1934

I

I have bought my ticket for Russia.

This statement, simple as it sounds, is as closely packed with complexities as the scientist's table is with atoms. Going to Russia, it appears, is almost as hazardous and complicated a business as going to Australia must have been in the days of Captain Cook. It is not simply a question of having enough money for the fare, as it would be if one were off to Paris, say, or the remote Bermudas. That is only the first necessity. An emigrant begging for admittance to a grossly over-populated country could hardly be more searchingly regarded than is the prospective tourist to Soviet Russia.

'A ticket to Russia, please.'

A group of Intourist officials scanned my face earnestly. It was evident that they recognized in me a notorious criminal. Would they give me in charge, I wondered. No. At least not yet. They would, however, keep me under strict surveillance. This I gathered from the glances which passed between them.

Which tour? A list was spread out before me and, still regarding me with suspicion, they told me that any of the set itineraries were available to me, but that I could not choose a tour other

15

than these without incurring considerable difficulty and more than considerable expense.

I brooded over the list, my mind swimming darkly round domes and towers, palaces and peasants, boyars, steppes, Tolstoy, the Red Guard, market places, the Imperial ballet—— Suddenly it came to rest and settled itself about three cities.

'What about Petrograd——' Dark basilisk eyes reproached me. 'I beg your pardon,' I said hurriedly, 'I mean Leningrad. Yes, and then Moscow —is it still Moscow?—and Nizhny-Novgorod. After that I should like, though it is not mentioned in this tour, to see Kazan.'

There was an ominous silence.

'It is not possible to see Kazan?'

'Not if you take this tour—no.'

'But in that case I shall take a tour that includes Kazan.'

'It is not possible.'

Shutters were down on all four faces. I felt daunted and somehow a little guilty. What had I done, what said? What was there about Kazan ——? Hurriedly, as one who has inadvertently mentioned something unseemly, I left the subject —evidently a thorny one—and began to discuss the fare.

'Then that's settled. You say there is a ship sailing on the ——th.'

They smiled pityingly. Did I think it was as easy as that? the concerted smile seemed to say. What then?

16

There was, it appeared, the question of fitting myself, or rather of being arbitrarily fitted by the Intourist officials, into a Tour. It seems that everybody goes to Russia in a Tour—it is against Soviet principles, if not Soviet laws, to travel about alone. The officials intimated that they would see to that. The assurance somehow failed to fire me with enthusiasm. But I was committed now. I must go on with it.

'You will fill up these forms.'

A sheaf of questionnaires, all identical, were handed to me. 'And a photograph for each. Yes. Then we shall see.'

So, I was on approval. Presently I found myself in the street clutching in one hand a pamphlet gaudy with towers, moujiks, workers and stray bits of machinery, with the words 'Soviet Russia —Home of the Free' blazing a trail across it, and in the other the collection of questionnaires— where was I born, of what nationality, what profession, color of eyes, etc, etc. Something has pricked the bubble of my elation. I am no longer the cheerful tourist but somebody who has asked for a job and is waiting for his references to be taken up. Not a human being, as I had mistakenly thought until now, but an entry in a 'T' file. Forlorn. Do they dam all springs at the source in Russia?

I have got my ticket. And my passport visa! I wonder what was the redeeming feature in those four photographs of a criminal lunatic (the cameras of passport photographers may not lie but they do a good deal of inventing) that spoke for me to the Consul—or whoever it is that gives passport visas. Anyway, I have been proved harmless enough to enter Russia for a period of some weeks. Perhaps the answers to the questions were sane enough to balance up the photograph. . . .

Take a gun! somebody said, but whether for the purpose of potting Russians or for myself should the Worse come to the Worst I am not quite sure.

Isn't it curious that nobody can hear even the name of Russia with any equanimity? Those for it are fanatically for it, those against it fanatically so. My forthcoming trip seems to be either the Chance of a Lifetime or a Piece of Utter Recklessness. If I had suggested a voyage at Arcturus I could hardly have caused more of a stir. This I should not mind if the enthusiasm and the disapprobation were not given such political significance. They have none for me, but then, though I am uncomfortably conscious that a person without a political ideal to-day is as inadequate as a cow with three legs, it is difficult for me to think or feel politically. Nobody, it appears, can conceive that a person who is admittedly neither for nor against the Soviet régime should want to go there. And it is an acid comment upon the Communist State that both sides are at one in their conviction that it is impossible for any one to go to Russia for purposes of enjoyment. The Anti-Soviets laugh heartily at such an idea, while the Pro-Soviets seem to suggest that if one has nothing better to do than enjoy one's self such a journey could only be a waste of time. In Russia, it would appear, Work is the great desideratum—work for work's sake, work for life's sake. Where have we heard these words before? Does it not seem to you that it has been drummed into us for the last two thousand years? Can it be that the new Russia is not so very new after all? Well, I shall know soon enough.

Thank you for the offer of a pair of skis, but though this is the second-last trip of the year I am told that such things will not be necessary. Besides, I have an idea that life is going to be much more serious than that. . . .

Now I know how the Pilgrim Fathers felt—cast away in their little punnet of a ship, desolate but proudly conscious of their super-stiff upper lips. I don't want to feel like this. The other passengers make me. 'Good-bye, good-bye,' as if we were setting out for Aldebaran. Everybody is being serious and solemn, 'Woikers,' professors, school teachers, business men and journalists. Russia, of course, is always news. 'The Russian cult is superseding the cult of the negro in England,' said one of them to me in headlines.

The Russian cult!

The North Sea is a dreary stretch of water—
Alfred Mond would have called it a waste—but
we hardly notice it. We are too busy talking—
groups of fanatically vocal cells crystallizing and
disintegrating. It's a sort of grand chain of conversation (or argument) where one never holds
the same hand for more than a moment. Is there
really so much enthusiasm in the world? Aren't
we forcing it just a little? I know I am. Lenin,
N. E. P., The Red Square, Komsomols, 1905—wonderful, too, too wonderful. Undoubtedly the new
religion, says the First Professor—oh, undoubtedly. . . .

'Yes, but what do you *do?*' said a School
Teacher, and looked pained when I said 'Nothing.' Why go to Russia, then? I am beginning to
wonder that myself—already. I feel so definitely
lacking in the right attitude. They all talk as
though it were the Holy Sepulchre. I feel the
Soviet is already too old and too set to be treated
like an infant prodigy among States.

'I hear,' said the Business Man from Man-
chester, 'that the best thing to see in Moscow is
the Kremlin's Tomb.'

The most favored people on the ship, with
crew and saloon passengers alike, are the 'woikers.'
They come up to the upper decks and talk to us
—or rather, at us. Very like the speeches in Hyde

Park, but better and truer, of course, because they are about Russia. I tell you, you don't know anything about Russia—except that Dostoievsky was born there. Do you realize that it is the only country in the world where a Jew can get work? Do you know that there is no hunger there and that every man is fed and clothed (and his wife and children) at practically no cost to himself throughout his life? Do you know that it was Lenin who said, 'Let there be light——'?

They have his shrine in the Red Corner, the mess room of the crew. A frieze of red-and-white slogans behind him, white immortelles grouped naïvely about him, the bronze god gleams in the swinging light, smiling rather sinisterly. They don't make obeisance to him—not yet.

Here, too, is the ship's cinema. It is thrilling to see Russian workers flickering mistily (the lens was very scratched) across the small screen, hordes and hordes of them coming out of one darkness and flying into another. But it is the machines, tenderly fed by more workers, that prompt our loud-throated Russo-British cheer. We are seeing life. Raw, red Russian life. Oh, boy, this is even better than the swamp! Not quite so good, but very moving, is the anti-bourgeois film that follows. The irrelevance of the last scene when the dark waters of the Neva engulf successively an armchair, a gramophone and a bottle of beer, is only apparent. Are not these the true bourgeois symbols? The First Professor was too moved to take up the trifling question whether the bottle was empty or not at the time of immersion. . . .

Somehow they have turned the ship into a kind of institution. Every member of the crew has the status of a sergeant-major. I lit a cigarette at dinner and had it whisked from my mouth and carried away upon a plate—a burnt offering to Soviet manners—and last night one of the school teachers left her napkin unfolded after dinner and she was brought back and made to put it neatly into its ring under the stern eye of a steward. She had just been explaining to me—we all explain to each other until patience gives out and then we frankly hector, the best lungs winning—that Communism was a Merging, simply a Merging, a losing of the Self in Something Greater. And it was disappointing to witness her grossly individual act.

The stewards and stewardesses, I am relieved to see, have solved this secret of merging. One only has to pass the galley unexpectedly to realize that.

'Have you noticed,' said the Business Man as we met on the companion-way this morning, 'that there seems to be more water on one side of the ship than on the other?'

I stared at him. Was it a joke, I wondered? It would be unlike him to make a joke.

'Have you?' he insisted, and went away looking depressed when I said that I hadn't.

22

Later in the day he came up to me with a perplexed look. 'It's funny,' he said, 'but now there seems to be more water on this side. I wonder why!'

He intends, he told me seriously, to see the captain and inquire into the matter. He seems to be even less well equipped for the trip than I.

The ship's book-shop harps rather upon one note. I have read three lives of Lenin, two volumes of his speeches, a selection from Stalin; and I now feel rather ashen, rather like one who for some time has listened to nothing but tom-toms. Surely there must be the proper antidote somewhere on the ship. But I cannot find it. Passing along the rows of deck-chairs the now familiar titles rear up and confront me: *My Life on a Collective Farm. Recollections of Lenin. N.E.P. Soviet Factories. The Young Octobrist. Work for All.* The ninety-and-nine and one gone astray. No, two. For the Poultry Farmer is not reading. He is photographing a dead sparrow that has dropped from nowhere on to the deck. Even the sea is withdrawn and unfriendly. It does not want to be looked at. It refuses to be the motive power of thought and dream. 'Merge!' it says sternly, whipping the ship's side with even, mechanical movements. 'Go and merge!'

'Would you like to read this?' says the First Professor beside me, and he hands me *The Year Book of the U.S.S.R.*

Kiel Canal. The ship slips through shining meadows that almost touch her sides. To anybody watching far away on those flat lands we must seem to be sailing on the land with the grass breaking in ripples at our prow. We are all being gentle to each other. It is the sea that has made us inhuman. Now we have stopped talking. Red and White lie down together like the lion and the lamb. Even the Russians and the Workers thaw to us a little. A sailor let me help him paint a railing yesterday, and at night I saw him stealing up the companion-way and very secretly going over my share of the work. . . .

The Baltic Sea is full of moons and stars. We can smell the North, a snowy, glittering, keen scent. Everybody is beginning to pack. My three dozen lemons have caused an unfortunate rift in the happy lute. You remember how we were told in London that a Russian (in autumn) will do anything for a lemon? When speech returned they told me to a man that there is no tipping in Soviet Russia, that the people themselves refuse to accept gratuities. I know, I know. All for love. But nevertheless I am glad I brought them.

Customs Office. Leningrad came towards us, swimming like a faintly colored water-bird over the flat swampy sea. It was a solemn moment when we drew into the quayside flanked by beautiful eighteenth-century chrome-colored build-

24

ings. Nobody degraded it with speech. We even remained silent when the stewards literally shoved us and our baggage down the gangway and soldiers propelled us without ceremony to the Douane. After all, there was nothing to say. They do not understand the English anathema and by the time our belongings had been thrown out by members of the G.P.U. and hurriedly re-packed by us we were convinced that we were guilty of some nameless but dreadful act. We are all criminals, and it is as well that we should know it. One soldier took all my papers to look at and read a letter from you with minute care. Halfway through he burst into a roar of laughter, but whether of rapture or contempt I could not say. He was reading it upside down. . . .

This is the most lovely city. At the first hurried glimpse the light, delicate houses and palaces seem strung like flowers upon the broad threads of the streets. The frost-blue, fire-blue Neva seems solider than its airy bridges.

Our hotel is very modern, very ugly, very new, and already the walls are peeling. It is suitably like a prison. It is bitterly cold both outside and in, but we are not going to have any tea. A dark, squat girl has arrived to take charge of us. We flock about her like starved sparrows round a crust. 'Now, what will you like to do? Yes? No? You can see, perhaps, the Prison Peter and Paul or the House of Culture for Workers.' A merry shout goes up and the party, blowing on its hands to keep warm, decides that either experience will be just too heavenly. . . .

It will take us four hours. Supper will be at ten or ten-thirty. 'Yes. No. I think, maybe we shall return in time for it.' Nobody ventures a pious hope that this will be the case. And if our thoughts are bleak nobody could guess it from our admirably composed faces. We eye each other searchingly. There are no signs of human weakness.

We are now setting out for the House of Culture. Holy Russia awaits us there. . . .

II

II

I WISH one could go about Russia alone. Being with a party and in charge of a guide is most demoralizing. One becomes lean and humble, and for one so entirely uneducated as myself the constant infliction of culture can be very tiring. It is so largely a matter of statistics. So many members, so many rooms, so many diversions, so many chances for the worker. The House of Culture to a man eyed us with astonishment. And no wonder. The spectacle of a group of people grimly determined to enjoy themselves at any cost is sufficiently curious.

It is hardly different from any Western Polytechnic, but because it was Russia we were shaken to our foundations. There was, of course, the anti-God lecture room. Zeus, we were led to believe, was going up in smoke and the Cross being bent into a cipher as we passed through, all very impressed.

The best part of it was the theatre. From a box perched high in the huge gloom we watched a group of workers rehearsing an opera. Under the green top-lights the stage, in all its undress, seemed set for some deep-sea tragedy, and the dark figures in dungarees swam slowly about in the aqueous glare, chanting sad briny songs. The director, who was leading our patrol, hissed something portentous into my ear. I appealed dumbly to the guide and she translated. ' 'E says—yes, it seats three thousand.'

We left him standing on the steps of the House of Culture still calling statistics after us. We were all humbled and silent. I felt like one cast away upon the ultimate shores of the world.

We are beginning to merge. The drabness, the universal grey, the complete sameness of the people is having its effect on us. We are infected with the need, obvious in all the Russians one sees, of living only with part of ourselves, of storing up precious energy and enduring, enduring, enduring. The machine is getting us, we are falling into place, cogs in the great wheel. We move from fortress to palace, from palace to factory with nightmare regularity. The great human clock goes ticking evenly, but nobody seems to know if it is telling the right time.

One has a lost feeling as though indeed we were in another planet. Here there is nothing familiar —even the people, grey themselves and only half visible in the grey northern light, seem to belong to a different star. The eye, indeed, of all the senses is the only one that is occasionally reassured. The eighteenth-century buildings continually draw one's thoughts home to something known and loved. The curve of chrome-yellow and white houses that confronts the Winter Palace is a dream of architecture. And from the square the streets lead off with almost musical precision and grace. As we huddle there, tossed by the North wind, with the sunlight-colored houses to the right of us and the monstrous marvel of the Winter Palace on our left, we are flanked by two worlds —eighteenth-century Europe and Russia, the form and discipline of one and the barbaric unrestraint of the other. The Winter Palace is an unforgettable sight, overgrown as it is with its lush untrammelled verdure of angels, cornucopias, urns. Thank God nobody read a riot act to its architects, nor constrained them to glance across the square and mark that foreign elegance. For the contrast is too perfect to be lost. Between these two extremes lies the great square, scene of the 1905 massacre and of countless others. The wind tosses backwards and forwards, now breaking on the yellow and white façades, now on the angels and the horns of plenty, and moaning wildly between them. A sense of death pervades everything. A city built upon the bones of the dead, its foreign splendor imposed upon, not growing out of, the level swampy land. Men lying dead under the wind——

'Let's go!' says the guide, and with a sigh of relief we fall into step behind her. It is outrageous to be tourists in such a place of tragedy.

I suppose all religions have their Bethlehem. The Russian variant is known as the Smolny Institute, but that rather drab title has a deep and solemn significance. Within its sacred walls the Republic was born. We stepped softly, going down the long corridor at the heels of the guide.

Somebody with a dramatic movement flung open a door and we found ourselves in a largish room furnished with rows of chairs, innumerable slogans and, behind the dais, a full-length portrait of Lenin with a background composed of a waterfall and an electric-light plant. Proudly the guide translated the slogan stretched across the top of the picture.

'Lenin says—"Communism, it is the Soviet plus electrification." '

'What does that mean?' I heard the Business Man ask the First Professor. The Professor's mouth, which had been open, closed hurriedly and the ecstatic light died away from his face. He looked dubious.

'It means—well, of course it means—er—exactly what it says—Communism is—er—yes, Soviet plus electrification.'

'Yes, but——'

'I think,' said the First Professor hurriedly, 'that we'd better be moving on with the others.'

The guide beckoned to us and, with some ceremony, marshalled us into an expectant group at the door of another room.

'Zis is the room where Lenin livvid,' she said

solemnly, and with such sincerity that one realized that nothing, not even successive relays of tourists nor successive explanations, could dim the splendor of that room for her.

Unfortunate Westerners! What gesture, what obeisance could we make without looking silly? To kneel would obviously not fit the occasion, and we could hardly cross ourselves. The First and Second Professors solved the problem for themselves by standing on tiptoe and continuing in that precarious attitude until the tour of the room was over. The others shuffled gently, speaking in whispers as they examined reverently the half bedroom, half living-room that Lenin shared with his wife after the republic was declared. The place was curiously moving. It may have been the bareness, it may have been the two narrow forlorn beds, or perhaps the grey light that drifted past the dripping birches through the large window. It was curious that emotions should be stirred in this place where emotion had been so rationally condemned. Such an emptiness was there, an emptiness that was not merely the lack of the room's inhabitant. Could it be that even when he lived there something was missing, some warmth, some central sun? Genius is light *and* heat. Had Lenin really that rare and twofold fire? Was it not rather a fierce and single light in which he burned? Consumed by mind—that is the impression one has when one looks at portraits and photographs of him. The only purely human quality in them seems to be a certain self-satisfaction, and amid such inhuman intensity one welcomes that with relief. At any rate it has the effect of convincing us—to some extent, anyway—that he was a man and not merely a mind on two legs.

But the chilliness of the place, the naked rationalism! It is difficult to believe that here a new world-force was set free. And if one does believe, it is with a kind of terror. Is this the point to which the human race has been rushing? If so, why have a human race at all—if its eventual aim is dehumanization? Men like gods? In this cold echoing air such an idea seems fantastic.

'It is made, yes, by Catherine ze Grit for a school for young noblewomen———' the guide is beginning again as she ushers us out of the holy of holies. Her voice, no longer gentle, is now edged with contempt, but the news is refreshing. I am glad to think the walls remember something a little irrational—laughter and the swish of satins and the nut-dropping sound of high heels, like the little hooves of goats, running along the corridors. What did they learn, I wonder, those young noblewomen? How to dress their hair in the latest fashion from Paris, to read and write in French and Russian? The intricate rules of elegant conversation were taught in this room, the arts of love, perhaps, in that. Perhaps Catherine herself came for the yearly prize-giving and chose the cleverest of them for her maids of honor.

But the guide has no time for any such wild

surmise and proceeds to tell us, like the good propagandist she is, that Catherine's predecessor, Elizabeth, left as legacy to the nation fifteen thousand dresses of diverse pattern and one rouble in the treasury.

Tch, tch, tch. We have no words with which to express our disgust.

(But I am wondering who got the rouble.)

To-day we were up earlier than usual to see the Summer Palace. It is grotesque and imposing, very long, and one imagines it stretching far back into the park, until one sees it sideways on and realizes that it is only one room deep. I suppose the game was to prevent the Ambassadors from foreign parts ever seeing it at that angle. The contempt of the guide for such an erection and for us for following her through it, is supreme. She was unintentionally sardonic in the picture gallery, when she gave the reason for certain discrepancies in the pictures. It appears that the gilt frames were put up before the world's masterpieces arrived so that in several cases the sizes of frame and picture refused to coincide. This difficulty was ingeniously overcome by adding to the too-small and trimming the too-large. Thus one may see a figure minus the outer edge of his left side from hat to boot, or a regiment of horsemen galloping headlong into a bunch of roses.

The trees of the park dropped their gold-leaf upon us as we walked across it to the Alexander palace where the guide achieved miracles of historical misstatement and the professors listened humbly as though, in spite of their knowledge, they believed it. A beautiful act of faith. Her habit is to give both question and answer and so save us the trouble.

Q. 'Who was Tsar Nicholas the late?'

A. 'Tsar Nicholas the late was a very stupid man dressed up in rich clothes.'

Chorus of Professors, Teachers, etc.: 'True, true.'

In Tsar Nicholas the late's study she flicked her head contemptuously at a row of silver horseshoes on the desk.

'Superstitious and unlucky, too.'

Poor man, he certainly was. And no wonder. All the horseshoes were wrong way up!

St Isaac's Cathedral is now an anti-God museum and its barbaric *décor* sorts well with its new career. A fanatic Director (every second person in Russia is a Director of something) built up a pyramid of proof of the non-existence of God. He showed us mummified bodies of shepherds and wood-cutters, conclusive evidence that one does not have to be a saint to retain one's person in perfection centuries after death; photographs of priests blessing Tsarist war-lords, the moral of which, since his English was rather on the Russian side, was not quite clear; instruments of ecclesiastic torture. His voice rose to a scream as he displayed the high peak of proof: a pendulum hung from the centre of the great dome that gradually changed its course after he had swung it for a minute. One gathered that the Bible had called the earth flat but that Galileo, Copernicus and others had by this simple experiment proved it round—*ergo*, there is no God. Nothing could have been more religious, more zealous for the faith, than this exposition. One sees at once that the Soviet is not concerned with atheism, but with throwing over one god to deify another—Man, perhaps, with the ultimate ideal Paradise, here and now, Heaven on earth, the symbol Lenin, and the choir of angels the Communist Party. There is no race more natively religious than the Russian—they have merely turned their faith in another direction.

(But the First Professor says all this is much too involved.)

We, since we travel hard class (and I tell you hard is a soft word to apply to it), go about in trams. These are always so full that the overflow passengers hang outside, the first row lucky enough to have a foothold on the step, the others hanging successively from the waists of these so that the trams seem to be bearing enormous bunches of grey grapes in their wake. (Earth-colored is nearer—earthenware people, newly made from swamp and steppes. The men would be handsome if they had more color, less of that

37

obliterating drabness; the women, sturdy with very short legs, seem mostly ugly, but I do not think I am really any judge of this.)

It is the women who wear best and who push hardest in trams anyway. They are, of course, better equipped for it, since it is a law in Russia that everybody, if he goes only one section, must enter the tram at the back, and push, fight, bruise his way through so that he may (if still alive) emerge at the other end. The women cleave a path by swinging the nether part of their bodies vigorously from right to left, and the sea, by some miracle, rolls back.

I *wish* I could go in a droshky. But they give us only six and something roubles to the pound, and the shortest journey costs ten roubles.

I have met T——. He came to the hotel last night and took me (and my pound of loaf sugar and three of the lemons) to see Z——: you remember him at Cambridge, the Russian anti-Communist? He shares his room with T——. And it is beautiful: a real fire, large old creaking chairs, soft with age; a chintz sofa with a pair of boots on it; Anushka, the servant, who actually smiles. Watch me thaw! My ears ache happily hearing real conversation again. The men sprawl on sofa and chairs. They are laughing! Honey, yellow and sticky as toffee and as thick! Wine in a bottle! White bread.

A young poet came in and read a long poem in

Russian about Aspasia, and Z—— and T——
translated it. It sounded good. But he can't get
it published because it isn't propaganda. What
good could Aspasia do the Soviet State? Cut off
her head!

He turned up again this morning with T——
and another man, a Russian, tall and sandily
middle-aged, with little light-blue eyes. I took up
my conversation with the poet where I had left
it off. He regarded me impassively. 'Not at all it
matters. I care only to write propaganda poems
for the Soviet World State.' I felt my eyes pop-
ping. But, you said—— I began.

'Come and see the cemetery,' T—— said hurriedly, and as he set off he pulled me behind the
others. The blue-eyed one was a member of the
Cheka. This person has, he himself told me as
we hung, the last layer but one outside a tram, a
passion for English literature, and several times
earnestly enquired if I knew Matthew Arnold
personally. I did not know whether this might
not be one of the Cheka standard third-degree
questions, and refused to give a definite answer.

I have always been morbidly fascinated by the
architectural exuberance of cemeteries abroad.
Père-Lachaise, for instance, has for me an antique
and pagan flavor, with its avenues of pretentious
and preposterous little houses for the dead. And
so the first burying place to which T—— and the
Cheka brought me had no air of strangeness. Deso-

late enough it was, with its tombs rifled, so the Cheka told me, for the metals that had gone to their making, and its graves thrown open by thieves in search of jewels and other treasures. But in spite of these ancient ravages the place had a tranquil elegiac air. One felt that here, at least, somebody was doing nothing. The caretaker (a courtesy title, obviously) had spread a few ragged clothes to dry among the tombs and the faint sun lingered lovingly upon the poor spots of color. We walked under trees that dripped recent rain from their shining leaves, and around our feet thick rank grasses and weeds swished musically. The dead, most of whom had yielded up their treasure, were now forgotten and nobody made a stand against that rampant surge of green. A poet of the romantic school would have loved it; and what joy it would have given, could he have possessed it, to one of those late eighteenth-century squires whose hobby it was to build ruined towers in their front gardens. We sat on a rifled tomb, with the green and yellow light dappling about us, the leaves dripping their gentle rain down the backs of our necks. The still place lapped us away from the monotonous movement of the city.

The Cheka wanted to know all about the life and personal preferences of 'Julian' Galsworthy and was shocked that we could tell him so little. When I remarked that I liked his cemetery he was still further disturbed. I had, I perceived, said

the wrong thing. This, he told me with some com-
miseration, was nothing. I must see the *Soviet*
cemetery. Now *that*, well, that was simply—but
he hadn't enough words. I must see it for myself.
He would lead the way.

The Soviet cemetery (only the best people are
buried there) is a masterpiece. It stands in the
grounds of the Alexander Nevsky monastery, and
at first sight looks like a Maori totem ground.
For the memorial to each of the dead symbolizes
his calling in life. Thus an engine-driver was sur-
mounted by a trio of traction-engine wheels looped
together with chains. Above the airman propellers
were erected; a soldier had a small imitation ma-
chine-gun. One grave was ringed round several
times with wire netting. I got the impression that
the occupant must have kept chickens.

The monastery was lovely, etched in the winter
sunlight. The faint gold stream from the birch
trees flowed over us. I forgot for a moment and
wished aloud that they had not turned its cloisters
into tenements. Cheka pounced upon me. Why
shouldn't the Workers have the best? And I
agreed. But then why shouldn't *everybody* have
the best? Not only the Workers—all kinds and
classes. There is enough and to spare. This seems
to me the only possible form of Communism. One
tires of all the snobbery about the Workers—
worse immeasurably than our snobbery of the
Upper Class. This Soviet State is pre-eminently

41

the bourgeois, class-ridden State. It *is* what it condemns. It is what we are pining to get away from, this and the mechanized age that it deifies. The Workers! How old-fashioned that sounds to us— Russia, in spite of its supposed newness and originality, is completely old-fashioned. It's in the Fifties, at latest the Nineties. They worship employment, and we, surely, are moving on to enjoyment. If not, what *are* we living for?.

All along the streets are food queues. The people stand quietly and greyly. Their endurance is so touching. Their faces have a steady, sealed look, as though they were under an anaesthetic. Is it hunger? Or are they, as the anti-Communists say, living on slogans, dreaming of the promised earthly paradise?

I met a woman in the Torgsin stores yesterday. She was grey and pinched, but there shone in her eyes that curious fanatical gleam I am beginning to know so well. She had been to America, she told me, and had returned to Russia after the Revolution. Her faith in the Soviet régime was supreme. 'We can endure the present,' she said proudly, 'for the time that is to come.' She answered my diffident questions expansively and friendlily. How was she so confident that a good time was really coming? What indication was there that it was approaching? Well—perhaps there were not so many indications, not at present. But they had only to wait. The promises would be redeemed. It was impossible that the Soviet State should fail. They must wait. Yes—they were often hungry, oh, and cold! But they mustn't grumble —hadn't they work? That was more than could be said for most countries in the world.

She talked gently, in a series of slogans. I begin to know them all very well. The most important of them is 'We have work.' Work! To the Western mind warmth and food is a compensation for work, but here work makes up for the lack of these. And I begin to see the reason for this. To have work in Russia, to be in a job, is to be socially significant. The moral effect of being of service to the State is inestimable, and the State is fully conscious of this fact and makes the most of it. The early Christians must have felt like this during the times of their persecutions. The righteousness of their cause filled their stomachs, and they warmed themselves at the fires in their own hearts. There is really very little difference. New Russia is preaching the same doctrine of denial. Meanwhile the earth groans under its plenty. Why should we not eat? The country that first sits down to the feast will lead the world.

The guide told me to-day that a woman tourist had once wanted to give her two pairs of warm stockings at the end of the tour. 'Imagine it! The insult!' And she is scantily dressed for this bitter weather! The will to endure. Or is it snobbery? I don't care. I like her. What the hell does it

43

matter if she's historically inaccurate? But how she hates us! I don't wonder.

Z—— tells me that they are so prolific that in fifty years they'll number 800 millions. 800 million workers. O lilies of the field!

III

III

To-DAY to the Peter and Paul fortress. Compared with the House of Culture I found it distinctly comfortable. Large rooms and windows, and resounding walls that must have given out a good echo when the political prisoners tapped out their autobiographies one to another. There were prisoners and warders in wax quite as good as Madame Tussaud's, and it saved us the bother of imagining them for ourselves.

In the little church by the courtyard stand the tombs of the Tsars, all exactly alike, and resembling a group of enormous paperweights. The guide's questions and answers are more elucidating than ever. To-day she began with:

Q. What is a tomb?

We all looked suitably blank. What *was* a tomb? She told us.

(Of course, I am being rather unfair. It is the tail-end of the season, and they are worn out after educating tourists all the summer.)

After recounting the circumstances of the deaths of Tsar Nicholas the late and his family, she remarked sternly: 'And if any one will tell you they was still leeving we will tell you that they was burned.' Finis.

I have discovered the reason for R——'s advice about corks. Do you remember he told me to be sure to bring several large ones? It seemed a curious admonition, but I brought some, nevertheless. I'm glad I did, for without them I could never have had a bath. You see, there appears to be some difficulty about making plugs in Russia. Or it may be that the baths were ordered from abroad and that the Western manufacturers, accepting the order with insufficient seriousness, failed to include the plugs. Or again it may be that the Russians, themselves not over-fond of water as an element, imagine that Westerners just sit under the tap and let hot or cold trickle over them and away.

But properly to introduce you to the bathroom you must first come through my bedroom. This is designed for the purpose of being all things to all men. The bed is in a curtained-off recess, and the rest of the room would appear to be an office. This is equipped with a large mock-walnut writing-desk, the kind usually associated with financiers in American films; a swivel chair in which, if I had a job to fill, I could swing round and terrify nervous applicants; two ordinary chairs (for the applicants to sit on, no doubt), and a small wooden set of drawers in which to file accounts and correspondence. In another corner, which doubtless forms the drawing-room of my establishment, is a solitary and unbearably durable armchair. My visitors, since there is only

48

one of these, are obviously not intended to sit down, or perhaps it is I who should stand up.

But the bathroom is the *pièce de résistance*. Its rich puce distemper is freckled with damp and there is a general rainy atmosphere about it. I cannot account for this, as the water is obtainable from the taps only at uncertain intervals. The chambermaid, more like a wardress in a mental home (and perhaps with reason, for it seems to me that we are all slightly mad), was horrified when I demanded a hot bath. Hot water is available only twice a week, she told me, the reason being that there is so little fuel for the furnaces. Ashamed of even having made the suggestion, I hurried to apologize and tentatively enquired if it would be convenient instead to encourage a little cold water to flow through the taps. But her manner suggested that even this request might better have been left unmade, and she went away jingling her keys. However, the porter, who made a valiant but ineffectual attempt to fix the electric light (the bathroom has been in complete darkness day and night since my arrival), has told me that the cold water may quite possibly come on to-night. I have my cork in readiness, anyway.

It will be lovely to leave Leningrad. In spite of its beauty it has a deathlike air. Its eighteenth-century perfection is a false growth; it rises so incongruously out of the flat swampy land. It is built of bones. Do you remember M—— describing to us the Nevsky Prospekt? It is now Prospect

October 25th and not one of those glories remains. Dark, horrible little shops, with a sparse muster of fur caps in the window or merely decorated with statues of Lenin and slogans, now fill those splendid buildings. The only shop we are allowed to enter, the Torgsin, is filled with the usual tourist horrors—Russian shawls probably from Birmingham, the crude legless wooden figures one sees in every arty-craftery in London, and, of course, 'the new Soviet Art'—boxes, china, medallions showing haloed tractors, winches and cranes. In these Torgsin stores they accept (perhaps take is the better word) English money, and if you consider all Russian transactions sacred and right (like the Professors) and do not protest, they give you as change dollars or guilders or pfennigs or cowrie shells.

Our conditioning continues. We are becoming used to living with only a minute part of ourselves. This is not, of course, admitted among us, but the contraction does occur, nevertheless. A certain sprightliness has gone from us. Where once we walked we now trudge. The light dancing step is subdued to a steady tramp. I am not suggesting that our spirits are less elevated, but the strenuous life is having its effect upon us all the same. The days, short in light, are long in time, and one is very like another. Eight-thirty finds us all seated round a long table, warming our hands round the teapots, talking with that spurious brightness

50

common at once to people who pursue the same object but are not really intimates and to those whose natural habit is to remain silent until the day is well advanced.

I came down the first morning to find the other members of the party assembled and looking rather pale.

'Is anything the matter?' I asked, perhaps rather tactlessly.

But they assured me with exaggerated brightness that it was nothing. As if anything could be the matter in Soviet Russia! But as soon as I sat down I knew. So I put aside the four eggs allotted to me (under the circumstances they can afford to be generous with eggs) and made my breakfast of cheese and bread and the inevitable *chi*—tea is a polite name for it.

Every morning it is the same. Some daring person, hoping against hope, cracks his egg and we all look the other way. But the cheese is marvellously sustaining—or rather sustaining enough for that small portion of us which now needs food.

Some such sustenance is necessary, for sightseeing begins directly after breakfast and goes on till about four or four-thirty in the afternoon. We then troop greyly back to the hotel for dinner—soup, meat-balls, potato and water ice-cream is the unvarying menu for this afternoon meal. The fact that this is a king's feast compared with the fare of the average Russian makes us stoical and nobody breathes a word of complaint. Once somebody forgot himself and cried lordlily for butter, and the moral vigor with which the rest of us denounced him would have been sufficient to start a new religion. But, since you are so far away, I can confess to you that I often wish I had an iron stomach, or that the human body, like the Ford car, could be fitted out with spare parts when necessary.

After dinner we stand at ease for about fifteen minutes or half an hour, and then we are off again till it is time to return to the hotel for our midnight supper—fish (of a kind) and, *mirabile dictu*, hot crossbuns! Every night, you see, is, as it were, Good Friday morning.

Some of us, the women members of the party, warned by the experiences of other voyagers to Russia, make tea in thermos flasks in the morning and bear these and slabs of chocolate with us to sustain us on our journeys. But the contempt of the guides when these are diffidently brought out cools the bourgeois brew, turns the chocolate bitter in the mouth and effectively reduces appetite. It is no good retiring to a sequestered spot to partake of the stimulants. There are no sequestered spots in Russia. One must either drink in public during a lull in manoeuvres or faint by the wayside. The iron-sinewed guides of course do neither, and I am beginning to feel, if one must do one or the other, that fainting by the wayside is a far, far better thing. In such an event one will get no pity—they tramp stray faces into the mud in Russia—but at least their contempt will be directed at one's physical inadequacy and not at one's principles.

Principles! *There's* a word. It assails the ear every other minute. Without principles in Russia you may as well be dead. Contrariwise, you may be as unprincipled as you like so long as you are possessed of Soviet principles. I begin to weary of the word, and to such an extent that I am thankful I did *not* bring that gun with me. . . .

Z—— took me to see the Rembrandts in the Hermitage to-day, darkly lovely in the half-day, half-electric light. I saw the elder brother of the boy in the Dublin National Gallery, or perhaps himself grown older, the curled lips firmer, the eyes more grave and showing himself more clearly. *That's* what one misses in Russia—the *person* in the eyes. The faces are so still and blank and the eyes glazed and empty. And dangerous, too, for one feels that any mood, cruel or fanatical, might blow in upon them and take up residence. One wants persons, not reiterated Soviet States.

It was snowing when we left Leningrad. T——, seeing me off, pushed a small sodden wad into my hands. When I opened it I found two hundred roubles. Half-heartedly, with visions of droshkies and green vegetables rising in my mind, I refused them. But he told me airily that it meant only two pounds to him as he lives and earns in Russia. When I bought hot coffee at one of the stations for two roubles, the party gaped in horror—six shillings for a cup of coffee! I longed to tell them that it was really only fourpence (or as really as anything can be with this Einsteinian exchange), but I had promised T—— not to say anything. For by this gift he and I have become members of the Black Exchange; we are defrauding the Government. It is a beautiful, almost a holy feeling. But I have gone up one with the party nevertheless. This is a paradox, for by rights they should hold me in contempt—a person who can spend six shillings on a cup of coffee. To the guillotine with her! But no—they are carrying my bag.

We spent the night between Leningrad and Moscow with a handful of comrades and about twenty soldiers. We lay, like a collection of preserves, on wooden shelves (oh, yes, of *course* a shelf each!) except for one of the soldiers, who walked up and down all night alternately singing and coughing. (The First Professor insisted on sprinkling me lavishly with a horrible thing called Insect Death. 'I have heard,' he said ominously, 'that in Russia——' and then moved on to pepper one of the School Teachers.)

The morning came at last. Dimly through the haze (double windows and all shut) we perceived the soldiers bearing down upon us, interpreter in hand. They wanted to know all about Britain. Did we intend to kill the King? Had we a large army? Did our soldiers (supposing we had an army) have meat every day? It was true, was it not, that the British Isles were 95 per cent Communist? Then *why not* kill the King? And the interpreter sat between us, a mild weather-cock blown upon in turn by Red and Pale Pink winds (for, really, the professors are no more than that, and I believe they are fading), repeating continually the everlasting double affirmative '*Da-da*' ('Yes-Yes') like a monotonous lullaby.

Outside the wet birches and pines went by, mile on mile of them, interminably flat. Nature *ad lib*. No limitations, no differences anywhere. The country seems half-made, and, like the people, mass-produced. Did somebody whisper in my ear, 'So many birch trees, so many pines, so many blades of green grass, so many of brown'? No, no, of course not. I am getting Directors on the brain.

Holy Moscow! How it bubbles, the onion-shaped domes are iridescent in the sunlight and at night they become faint luminous spheres among the stars. It is an astonishing city, rather like a gigantic film set. It is difficult to accustom one's self to this Eastern passion for the circle. I felt it vaguely in Leningrad, but much more definitely here, this Eastward movement of Russia. Widdershins, anti-clockwise, against all reason when one remembers that the rest of the world is marching steadily to the West.

The people are still drab, the color still to be found only in churches and towers, but Moscow

has a more lively air than Leningrad and the enthusiasm for work is even more marked. We have
changed guides. This one is large and blonde and
less baleful than the last. But she dragoons us
like a sergeant-major. Her 'Let's go!' is only another way of saying 'Quick march, and you there,
keep in step!'

We are not to be allowed into the Kremlin.
THEY are sitting—that's the excuse. But surely,
the Kremlin's so enormous. Couldn't THEY sit in
one part of it and let us see the rest? No, THEY
are sitting all over it—discussing, I gather, Soviet
Propaganda in Foreign Parts, and the cry of the
tourist is not to be heard in the land. So we are
condemned to walking all round the red crenel-
lated walls that give one such a sense of cruelty.
Indeed, Moscow as a whole is cruel, the shape
and color of it, as it lies about its dark river and
climbs the Kremlin hill. And the high bland voice
of the guide accentuates this impression. 'These
is where Tsar Ivan murder his son. These is the
stone of the felons—they are chained to these
ring. Yes. Let's go.' (Professor, I think you are
out of step. But he says that *I* am.)

They keep us out of the churches, we are to see
only the outside of the glittering onions. In-
variably we are told that the churches are closed
or being turned into gymnasiums. But yesterday
I slipped behind the guide when she was teaching

history to the poultry farmer and went in through a mosaic door to candle-lit darkness. A service was in full swing and the church was packed. A shape detached itself and moved like a ghost towards me. She was wrapped in the usual nondescript clothes, her feet bound with rags to the remains of a pair of shoes. She began to talk in French with the rapidity of fear. It was unbearable. I gave her some of my roubles and she thrust them quickly away among the rags and fell on her knees again. It was rather a relief to be able to give something—this vast snobbish refusal to receive withers the heart. 'Oh, we absorb them!' the guide said airily, when I asked her later what had become of the old Russians. Well, I suppose absorb is as good a word as another.

This business of liquidating the churches in Russia is obviously one of the first articles of the Soviet faith. The guides find our interest in such bourgeois relics very galling, and they are never tired of making uncomplimentary remarks about their evil influences. On more than one occasion a church in the process of being demolished has been pointed out to us with ill-concealed triumph, and we have, I think purposely, been shown others that have become offices or clubs or gymnasiums. Interest in a church—even if only for the sake of its architecture—is condemned as Tsarist ideology and as such is sternly suppressed.

The Business Man, however, has discovered in

himself a genius for finding churches that are still used for their original purpose. He is, I discover, a churchman himself and takes round the plate in his parish chapel every Sunday at home. At first he made it his business to report his discovery to the guides, less out of a desire to inform on the unfortunate church than to enjoy a poor moment of triumph and victory. But he has now been persuaded of the tactlessness of the manœuvre even though it may prove the guide a liar. He is now content to beckon silently and mysteriously whenever he has news to communicate, and this he does with such energy and excitement that it is quite impossible for the guides to mistake his meaning.

'Little chapel!' he whispers loudly and with an overplus of breath into the nearest ear. 'Just down road—full of ikons—two priests holding service—packed! You must see it!' And the guides make a mental note of it for the next Cheka meeting.

Last Sunday he came in to luncheon garlanded with smiles, his secret boiling up and overflowing.

'Another?' I enquired. He nodded.

'But not one of those Russian affairs. A real church—Lutheran—and *such* a pleasant service!'

Our Russian education has a curious curriculum. To-day our first port of call was a crèche. The professors marched in two by two with that fixed air of interest which has become habitual to them. In an antechamber we were forced into white overalls. As these were all the same size and we were not allowed to take off our overcoats you can imagine what we looked like. Thus apparelled we trailed through a series of nurseries. The details made the professors distinctly embarrassed, I was glad to see. In the room for two-year-olds several very small old men were seated round a table trying hard not to spill their gruel on their pinafores. They were grave and sombre, very conscious of the red slogan that stretched across the room. The guide translated it. 'Play is not just fun. It is the preparation for toil.' There, little ones!

On one wall hung the portrait of an ethereal little boy in a frilled silk shirt and blue velvet trousers. A nimbus of yellow curls shone about his head. To my raised eyebrow the guide said raptly, 'Lenin as a leetle child.' The old men gazed sombrely up at it, their spoons poised in mid-air. The apotheosis has begun.

It was not a very clean crèche, and I couldn't help wondering if the overalls were to protect the babies from us or us from the babies. The latter, I think.

Who was St Basil? They have built him a Cathedral overlooking the Red Square. I won't say it is in the worst possible taste, for there is no taste there at all, simply horror heaped on architectural horror. And, very suitably, they have turned it into an anti-God museum. Very like

St Isaac's, except that it lacks the pendulum, but it possesses a poster that St Isaac's may well envy. I found it in one of the smaller chapels, a very gaudy, very gorgeous representation of the Soviet version of St George and the Dragon.

At the bottom of the picture, members of the proletariat are shown writhing in the coils of an enormous monster, fire-breathing, iron-clawed. A little higher several top-hatted devils (obviously bourgeois devils) add sauce to the occasion by poking the proletarians deeper into the monster's embrace with spears and tridents. But help is at hand. Crowning the picture, in the pure blue day-shine, comes the deliverer, hero-light about his head, and behind him the heavenly host. The crowned head is Lenin's, and one can distinctly make out the followers, Stalin, Kalinin, Molotov, etc. No wonder the White Army is bolting out of the picture, to the right, as fast as its horses can carry it. The whole thing has the quality, not artistically, but in feeling, of some early painting. I hate to confess it, but it makes me think the First Professor must be right, and the thought is an uncomfortable one. The New Religion!

T—— has written to ask if I will go with him and Z—— to Novgorod in the Ukraine, but though I have gone to the most lamentable lengths of threat and cajolery, Intourist won't let me. My tour is for Leningrad, Moscow and Nizhny-Novgorod, and the Volga, and it cannot be altered.

But why? They give no reason—it cannot be done. But if I need no guide, since T—— and Z—— both speak Russian and will look after me—? No. It's no good. Mine not to reason why. This *prison*! Russia is a vast negation. Ask and it shall be refused.

And *all* your letters to me have been opened. I *won't* stand it. (It doesn't make it the least easier to know that I've got to. But, you know, even as I say this, I'm thinking—unrestrained individualism is almost as bad as no individualism at all. But I'm only thinking it in my mind. My heart and all the other centres of thought stand steady for identity. I think it's the professors and the desire not to be entirely reactionary that engender these plain thoughts.)

IV

IV

THE happiest place I have yet seen in Russia is
the Moscow prison. No, but seriously. I know I
should quickly gravitate there if I lived in Russia.
It was Sunday, or rather the Fifth day, the equiva-
lent of Sunday (the Lord rested on the fifth day
in this country), and so there was no work being
done. That in itself was sufficiently refreshing and
novel. After half an hour of statistics (five to ten
years for murder, prisoners allowed out on parole
during the harvest, less crime in Russia than anywhere else, etc, etc), the Director loosed us among
the prisoners. None of them seemed to be locked
up, some were lying in their bunks—four berths
to a cell like a ship's cabin, and the walls decorated
with paper cuttings and the inevitable prints of
Lenin and Stalin—others were moving about carrying bedding, and some were simply doing nothing. It was very dirty and very homely and every
face had a look of joyful triumph. And why
wouldn't it? The individual anti-social act that
had brought each one there must have, at any
rate for a time, set him free, cleansed him from
the mass in him. An individual act in Russia cor-
responds, I should think, to a drinking bout in
the West. It is the fire that purifies.

I keep on remembering, of course, the ghouls

65

at home who repeat the old axiom, 'Ah, but they only show you the best!' But there was nothing very model about this prison, it was the men themselves who struck me. And surely even the best of Soviet States could not impose a natural happiness upon a mixed group of people for the benefit of stray tourists.

Nor was the boot factory a model one in the Western sense of the word, nor the crèche. Factories, crèches, prisons—doesn't it sound to you the most lunatic kind of nightmare? Not one of us would put foot inside such places in the West (unless impelled by no will of our own into the last), and yet here we are, solemnly trooping about looking at boots, babies and criminals as reverently as though they were bits of the true Cross. We are partaking of the Russian cult.

It was inevitable, after the prison, that we should see the courthouse. Having shown us the criminal in full bloom, as it were, Intourist would have felt it was not doing its duty had it not shown him to us in the making. So we stowed our note-books in our breast-pockets and set out.

'The Russian judicial system is the finest in the world,' declared the First Professor as we entered a murky room furnished with a few forms and a dais. We took our seats upon the forms (Could you move along a little, Professor, I am right on the edge!), and presently to us entered a severe-looking youngish man and two young women whose expressions by comparison made that of the man seem positively seraphic.

Plaintiff and defendant then emerged, the former a wizened little old man with a peering, dusty, birdlike face, wrapped round with an off-white handkerchief. The defendant, a blue-eyed young giant, filled the court-room. It seemed to tremble at his hugeness, and to be ready, if he moved, to collapse and make way for him. He stood there, truculent and sheepish, his great hands curling in and out of each other behind his back.

One could see at a glance what had happened. The old man had got on the wrong side of the giant and the giant had socked him one—or rather several.

The man on the dais, a magistrate evidently, began to question the plaintiff, who poured out a lengthy whine of abuse, his eyes turned away from the huge creature at his side. As he talked he edged a little towards the dais, as though, even now, he needed protection from his assailant. The two young women looked down upon them both with equal ferocity.

'''E says,' whispered the guide to some one at the end of the row, 'the young man got drunk on vodka and beated 'im up.'

'''E says the young man——' the whisper is repeated all along the line and the remark is transferred to all the pocket-books.

In an enormous voice the giant began his defense. The walls trembled. So did the plaintiff.

The guide whispered again and the disclosure trickled along the line until it came to me, sitting at the end. My neighbor, the Second Professor, whispered it hurriedly so as not to miss any of the scene himself. I could only make out one word and it didn't sound right somehow.

'Boot? Did you say boot?' I hiss into his ear.

'Flute!'

'What flute?'

'Tch, tch, tch!' says the Second Professor. 'I said it distinctly enough—he played the flute.'

'Who did?'

The Professor is clearly exasperated.

'The old one!' Regardless of the fact that he is in a court of law he hurls the remark at me.

'O-o-h, I see. Thank you.'

My sympathies, with the giant from the first, were now richly increased. No wonder he had 'beated up' the old one. Think—perhaps he had listened to that flute for years, and for years had held his hand. The same tune over and over again —not even a tune, perhaps, just a series of notes. And then a lucky chance had put him at the head of a vodka queue. He had taken his bottle and had gone home to drink it ruminatively to the last sweet dregs. After that he felt he must rid the world of its horrors, and he had begun (and alas, ended) with the flute-player. It was an altruistic gesture, and one worthy of a giant. I had no doubt that he would be let off with a caution.

68

But the three magistrates looked very unbending as they discussed the case.

'Zeese,' I could hear the guide explaining, 'are the fellow-workers of the defending. It is zeese will judge him. A worker is judged by the fellows. Yes.'

Indeed he is. Judgment was printed in large letters on the faces of the fellows. The man spoke, delivering the sentence. There was a little pause at the end, and the giant clenched his hands fearfully, and then with complete calmness he went out, truculent but resigned. The plaintiff followed at a safe distance looking still older and a little depressed.

'What happened?' We crowded round the guide, pencils poised expectantly.

''E—the young one—is discovered guilty. 'E will pay the half of his wages for one year to the Party funds and to prison for one month. Let's go.'

Oho—so that's how the Party gets its sustenance! It seems an excessive penalty for what must have been a moment of pure pleasure.

'Are you sure the guide said half his wages for a whole year?' I asked the First Professor. For reply he showed me his note-book. The fact was neatly written down.

Sunlight was speckling the cobble-stones as we walked home. The First Professor, basking in it, had forgotten the scene in the courthouse. In that unguarded moment I asked him:

'What would you get, Professor, in the West, if you gave me a black eye and I took the matter to court?'

'Oh, ten days hard or a couple of quid——' he began lightly, and then catching my eye he broke off hurriedly. 'Or—er—probably more. Really, I can't say. Different conditions, you know—judicial system not the same—impossible to judge—quite impossible——'

'I see,' I said simply. And the Professor saw that I saw.

To-day I saw V——, who is sharing the curtained-off end of a passage with another girl, sleeping on the floor and fetching water from another building. And she is not only happy but ecstatic. What *is* it? Does she feel herself part of some moving thing, some stream of new and glorious life that eludes us? Or does she only *think* she is, as a result of the slogans in the air? Oh, well, it's the same thing anyway.

Definite signs of strain are noticeable among us. We all snap at the slightest provocation, but I am still the outcast, the irreverent one. To-day, coming back, the Third Professor stood up suddenly in his seat in the omnibus and cried, 'I can't stand it, I can't stand it! I must go up on to the roof and sing "Land of Hope and Glory"!' The horror on the faces of the rest at this exhibition and at the malicious gleam of triumph in my eye

70

beggars description. Two of them thrust him back into his seat muttering that he must pull himself together (for the honor of the regiment, I suppose), and they then excused him to me by saying that he was drunk! So the incident passed, but it has left a slight breach. And the Third Professor always finds something of enthralling interest on the opposite horizon whenever I appear.

Outwardly, however, the merging goes on. Pedantically we call each other Tovarish or Comrade to make our surroundings more real to us and ourselves more at one with them. Everywhere in the streets one hears the word scattered through conversations. It has usurped the Little Father-Little Brother of an earlier period, but Russia has not escaped from Dostoievsky yet, with its mixture of ecstatic emotional merging and mindless brutality. I saw two men casually quarrelling in the street the other day, and one suddenly leapt at the other, flung him down and ground his face into the mud with his foot. Little father, little brother, love one another. I killed Ivan because he stole my penknife.

To-day we have been to what the Business Man still calls the Kremlin's Tomb. It stands beneath the walls of the Kremlin in the centre of the Red Square, which is beautifully proportioned. The tomb itself, of onyx (I think) and red granite, is like most modern monuments in Russia, massive and paperweighty. All day long queues wait outside, moving foot by foot very slowly to the entrance, which is guarded by soldiers.

Led by the guide we lagged at the tail end, pressed in against the silent shawled figures. Extraordinarily silent, not merely not talking but silent within themselves. One felt, waiting there with them, that one shared their purpose, and was clear and open for the mystical experience that obviously it was to be for them; ready, even eager, to be impressed by this dead but living god.

From the entrance steps open downwards lit by a diffused red electric radiance. They wind a little before leading into the darker and redder vault. Nothing that could heighten the dramatic effect has been left undone. The crowds moved silently past the still little figure on its red cushions under its glass case. But the nothingness of that figure was pitiful, a statue of poor flesh preserved against its own will and against all law. It wasn't death, which is dynamic and immediate. It was nothing. The resolute materialism of the Soviet State finds its end in this. This emptiness could not move one except to anger, perhaps, against those who defrauded a great man of his body's disintegration and made it a thing for tourists to gape at and peasants to pray to. But the humble voice of the soldier who gently took my arm and guided me through a dark place on the stairs was moving and full of beauty, it was life pulsing and flowing in that place of mock heroics and sham death; it was a challenge.

'Most impressive! *Most* impressive!' said the Second Professor, and gave me a warning De Mortuis look as though he were afraid I was going to make some comment. But I wasn't.

You were quite right to give me that letter to the cinema studio. It has enabled me to have my senses beaten black and blue (if such a thing is possible). And to meet the most extraordinary young man from Birmingham who has gone so Bolshie that even the Bolshies think him rather too much on the Red side and are trying to cool him down. I need hardly tell you that he is a Director. To-night for my benefit he screened the preliminary pulls of the new film he has made of Magnetogorsk. His conversation is wild to the verge of being unintelligible, but I gather that this is some enormous plant which is to be the envy of the world as soon as the world hears of it. And his film is preparing to tell the world. None of the sound effects have been incorporated yet, but he had provided as understudies a huge tin drum, a wooden rattler, a large church bell, a motor siren and his own powerful voice. The film swarms with young Russians, Komsomols is the word, all, apparently, with the utmost venom, trying to do the next person out of a job in order that he (or she) may do it himself. It sounds

73

fantastic, I know. But it *was* fantastic. Then there were the Kulaks—'Class Enemy!' roared the Director, and blew a fanfare on the siren. 'Setting fire to the plant in revenge. Look, real flames. I did that!' But the Komsomols, judging by the energy they put into clanging the bell (neatly synchronized at my right ear by the Director), were up to all class-enemy dodges. They paused only to kill a few class-enemy babies (the puling cries of these echoed in the siren) and then got to work on the Class-enemy himself, with the maximum of noise. 'They know all Russia is looking to them!' the Director bawled and gave the tin drum several resounding kicks. 'Get it?' he enquired. I could only nod. Indeed I got it. 'Dramatic, what?' he roared.

And, you know, it was—in a wrong-headed sort of way. Intensely dramatic. The climax came when several thousand (or so it seemed) Komsomols took triumphant possession of the plant (tin drum, church bell, siren, rattler and Director proclaimed it) and set to work again. The last scene showed several female Komsomols strenuously wheeling enormous barrows of coal (or iron or lead) up a steep incline—an allegory, I suppose, suggesting the path to Heaven.

'Equal rights for both sexes in Russia. Triumph of Woman!' the voice of the Director, rather sandpapery now, summed up enormously. Then silence descended. We were both so moved we could not

74

speak for a minute. Then he asked me didn't I think it effective, and I said that I did. . . .

The studio is some miles out of Moscow, and when he had locked the door behind us he pointed out a minute glitter of light on the horizon. 'That's your tram,' he said briefly, and I surmised that he was not going to sink to any bourgeois level and take me home. I was right, for before I could reply he was walking away briskly in the opposite direction as energetically as any Komsomol.

It was very dark and eerie and lonely waiting for that far-off tram, but I was too bruised to care. I kept hearing the Director's voice like a knell—Barrows of lead, freedom of sexes, triumph of woman. Barrows of lead, freedom——

Could you, without much bother, send me a nice comfortable pair of shackles?

V

WE continue to move in a body, like some faint, cooling sun through strange Zodiacal signs—the House of Culture, the House of the Workers, the House of Sports, the House of Prostitutes——

To the last I refused resolutely to go. The guide did all she could to persuade me and couldn't believe that I wasn't in the least interested. I notice, by the way, an increasing repugnance on the part of the Intourist guides to my occasional absences from the tours. They regard me with blank disbelief when I say I want to meet my friends. Can it be that they think I am secretly engaging in Subversive Propaganda? And if so, shall I not hear shortly, above what remains of me, a voice (probably the First Professor's) husk-ily saying 'Cover her face; mine eyes dazzle; she died young'?

The rest went off rather sheepishly, pretending they were doing it as a matter of duty, a mere question of form. As indeed it turned out to be, for they returned to the hotel very disappointed, having seen nothing but row on row of statistics. And on such an occasion statistics are apt to be rather inadequate, even for the Professors.

It is bitterly cold now and unless one retires

to bed it is almost impossible to get warm; owing
to the scarcity of fuel the central heating of most
buildings is rather decentralized. To-day we went,
huddling together like shorn lambs, to the Trety-
akoff Gallery. It is customary in the West to give
up one's bag, one's stick and one's umbrella before
going into the Tate or the National Gallery. In
Russia, however, where people are more thorough,
overcoats are removed as well. In case (I suppose)
anybody should try to get past the commissionaire
with a canvas hidden about his person. I cannot
think even the most eccentric visitor to the Trety-
akoff would have wanted to do such a thing. None
of the pictures are of the kind one would want to
live with. Indeed, we were not expected to admire
the pictures as such; it was their grouping that
was designed to impress us. You see, they were
arranged according to Soviet Principles. Thus, one
room would be filled with a jumble of paintings of
rich nobles; silks, satins, laces and jewels frothed
about us on all sides, filling us with languor and
satiety. And then—the guide's face was a whole
melodrama—we were switched into a gallery cram-
med with peasants undergoing every kind of torture. Sensational is hardly the word. Life, for
nineteenth-century Russian artists, could not have
had a dull moment. *They* needed no *vie de bohême*.
The bourgeois gallery was good, too, with its reiterated young girls being offered to reiterated
lecherous old men by reiterated soulless parents.

80

You know, I have arrived in Russia at the wrong moment. I should have come in the *eighteenth* century when, judging by these pictorial accounts, things were more lively. I did not speak of this, however, for I could see that it was not an occasion for flippancy, and the expression on the faces of the professors told me that if they had been wearing hats they would have reverently removed them. . . .

I have seen Stalin. Or rather I may have seen him, the chances being six to one against. An enormous Rolls flicked past us as we were trudging back to the hotel and I caught a glimpse of a dark Asiatic face huddled in one corner. Somebody said 'Stalin!' But by that time all we could see was the back wheels of the car. The guide said it might be he and it might not; she was not prepared to commit herself. But I understand that six Rolls-Royces each containing a dark Asiatic face huddled in one corner leave the Kremlin every night and return to it the next day and that nobody (not even the chauffeurs) knows whether he has seen Stalin or one of the five understudies. There are, of course, no would-be assassins left in Russia, but, if there were, this ruse would hardly give them a dog's chance of spotting their man.

I wonder what it is exactly that determines Intourist's choice of our daily programme. What mind, for instance, conceived this morning's itinerary? I am still pondering this question. This is what we did:

From a steep flight of concrete stairs we stared out, like frozen rooks from their tree-tops, at a flat expanse of land which was sparsely ringed about with aeroplanes. We were not allowed to come within yards of these, however, it being considered sufficient entertainment for us to shiver on the ramparts and watch Moscow in the distance being swallowed up by a grey mist. This was called 'seeing over the aerodrome.' The guide's signal for departure was never so swiftly nor so eagerly acted upon. As we left, a giant Fokker plane, as if out of pity for us, circled the landing-ground and landed neatly and dramatically. It looked like some gigantic malevolent insect with its great ringed eyes and pointed tail. As soon as it touched the earth two men sprang out of a little window at the top and waved Russian flags vigorously. A frosty wind carried our faint cheers to them. We were grateful—they had given us a semblance of a reason for our presence there.

But there was no adequate explanation for our attendance, half a hour later, at the sports ground —a smaller Wembley and just as desolate.

'This ees Stadium,' says the guide flatly.

We regard it steadily and with distaste. We touch the wooden seats. Yes, she is quite right. It is a stadium. But it is difficult to comment suitably upon this fact. The Business Man semi-saves the situation by asking, more from habit than interest, one feels, how many people it accommodates. The guide consults the Director of the Sports Ground (who has of course accompanied us since we first entered the gates) and elicits from him just how many thousands arrive for every event. Notes are taken. We pass out with our usual jubilance not so much in evidence. An empty stadium is the very soul of emptiness. Even the Professors have nothing interesting to say about it, no questions to ask. At the most it has served to add an entry to the others in the notebooks. But unless we, as a party, are preparing to raid Moscow from the air or to form ourselves into a football team with the intention of challenging the Moscow Wanderers, I cannot see that our knowledge of modern Russia is in the least increased by this morning's festivities. I suppose Intourist—our mother for the moment—knows best. But it is hard to believe it.

My roubles are going—on droshkies and lettuces. The latter I share with the party so that we usually have a leaf apiece. At first they were adamant and refused such bourgeois consolations, and stuck manfully to our daily diet of—well, it tastes like horse and whale. But since I told them that the lettuces were bought for medicinal rather than luxury-trade reasons it has been all right and they share with me. All except the Poultry Farmer. This at first astonished me, for he is not

83

pink at all but brightly painted in red, white *and* blue. Then I discovered that he has sold a (spare) pair of trousers to a needy Russian for sixty roubles and that he buys his own lettuces and eats them in solitary grandeur when everybody else is asleep. By the way, when I say needy, I mean a Russian who needs a pair of trousers, not one who is indigent. As a matter of fact they have money, all except the Old Russians, that is, but there is so little on which to spend it. V—— took me to see a family, six of them in one room, who don't know what to do with the money they earn. And they are very nearly starving. They showed me a pile of meat tickets inches high, but since there is no meat available these are no use to them whatever. Here, you see, is the reverse of our Western dilemma, poverty in the midst of plenty. But in Russia the plenty is money and the poverty lack of produce. So that both civilizations—I *beg* your pardon, *cultures* (one could hardly call the Soviet State civilized and if one did it would be offended)—seem in different ways to be mistaking the nadir for the zenith.

I have been to a wedding—we have all been to a wedding. And to two divorces. These all occurred inside fifteen minutes, so you need hope for no details about orange blossoms or what the judge said when he granted the decrees nisi. There was nothing bourgeois like that. These were up-to-date modern affairs, quick and effective as a zip fastener. They were as magical and as complete

84

as the transformation scene in a pantomime, and they only cost a rouble—at least the wedding did. I'm not sure about the divorces—probably a few copeks.

There is the registrar—a stern woman (all the women officials are very stern in Russia) with lank hair and an expression of extreme efficiency. There are the bride and bridegroom. Your name, please. And yours! So. And there is the rouble. The thing is done. Next, please.

The divorces consisted of two post-cards. So far as we could see there were no persons attached to them. The guide explained that in order to get a divorce one party to the marriage only need apply. He, or she, simply sends a post-card to the registrar telling her that she (or he) wishes to be married no longer. It is like the Arabian Nights. You wish and your wish is fulfilled. It is not even necessary for the party (the word is the guide's) bringing the divorce to consult the second party. So, you are quite likely to wake up one morning and find that you are no longer a husband or a wife. It is courteous, of course, to inform your wife, or your husband, of the divorce proceedings, but even this does not seem to be absolutely necessary.

It was so easy—snip-snap, and all over—that I felt there must be a catch in it somewhere. And there is. The catch is the child. In the event of divorce each of the parents is severally responsible for it until it reaches the age of eighteen. When I heard this I found myself, unequivocally, believing the guide when she informed us that divorces under the Soviet régime are 15 per cent fewer than those under Tsarist rule.

But in marriages where there are no children there is no end to the number of times you may be married and divorced. A young American I met a few days ago told me that a friend of his, also an American, had given an old gramophone to a Russian girl before he returned home. She was conspicuously plain in person, but she was immediately married by a young man with a taste for music. As soon as he had gained possession of the gramophone he divorced her and married a prettier girl. Succumbing, he made his new wife a present of the gramophone, and upon that she divorced him and married a handsomer husband. And so on. The gramophone led a giddy life, passing from marriage-bed to marriage-bed. Its end is not recorded. Probably it died eventually of old age and overwork. . . .

Grey, grey, grey—nothing but grey on the faces of the people and in the whole width of the sky. Oh, where is Genghiz Khan? We should be hearing rumors of him and we so far in the East. Last night I asked the First Professor to come with me in my droshky and look for him. He hesitated, but I will not do him the injustice of saying that he hesitated long. It was against his principles: he had undertaken to travel hard class and travel hard class he would. I dare say Adam felt like that about all fruits other than the apple. And I know now how he must have looked when it was stretched out to him, the slow tides of light rising in his eyes, steadily brightening and expanding, threatening to engulf him and no hand near to save him. But the First Professor was luckier than Adam. One of the School Teachers flung him a straw. There was to be a lecture on *Hamlet* Interpreted According to Soviet Principles by a Mr. Bloomberg in the hotel. But suddenly the Professor, with a reckless gesture, decided to drown and climbed into the droshky.

Of course we didn't find Genghiz. I knew the Professor was not seriously looking for him but merely accepting him as an Excuse for Propaganda. Driving through the beautiful sleety streets with the domes like smoke-rings in the air, he had no thought but for my conversion. I was missing, he said, the Whole Point of the tour, and that really, with an Intelligent Woman's Guide to Communism literally spread out before me, not to take advantage of it was——

And so, of course, I had to come back from Genghiz Khan and you (I am getting frightfully homesick—are you still alive, have you grown a beard, it is all so long ago and far away!) and try to convert him. I explained to him as best I could —isn't it remarkable to have reached his age and not to know it?—that woman is naturally communistic and that for her to become politically so is simply gilding the lily—or, if you like, de-gilding it. How is it possible (I asked him) to lock one's self up in a moment of time with *Finis* written on the outside? That's what he's doing. The whole Russian experiment seems to me to be much too important for us to regard it as though we were a row of chickens with the gapes.

'Important? Ah, you admit that?'

Of course, I admit it. But at the same time it seems to me horribly imperfect, horribly old-fashioned, horribly bourgeois (My God! exclaims the Professor, forgetting that the exclamation itself proclaims him an indifferent student of Soviet Principles), and at the moment more like Tom Brown's Schooldays or a Church Lads' Brigade than an ideal State. If I regard this as ideal I must exclude everything else, and if I exclude how can I be a communist in any ultimate sense, a communist in the true meaning of the word? A part is not enough for me, I want all.

It is astonishing to me that the Professor is astonished.

This little group of intellectuals—all their history, all their knowledge, all their sense and imagination has flowed away from them. Indeed, they have deliberately committed acts of sabotage and sprung leaks in their own minds in order to be able to look at Russia untrammelled by any sense of proportion. All this I told him and more—at decent intervals—for he has a habit of mistaking me for a large class of students in a lecture-room and talks as one used to having the dais to himself. Still—on the whole he was fair and let me have my turn. Neither of us won—and indeed I didn't really want to win. I realize I must be a dreadful thorn in his intellectual side.

Too much sleet. I have been in bed all day with influenza, and to-night the F.P. has sent me a tiny bunch of flowers. Where he got them I do not know for there isn't a flower in Moscow. When I thanked him he said surlily that it wasn't kindness but pity for my political ideals!

I missed the lecture on Hamlet but I have been to see Hamlet himself. And I want to know why, why, why I was not taken first to the theatre instead of to Houses of Culture and the like. One of us is a lunatic—me or Intourist—and I can't think it is me. Never mind about grammar now, I must talk about the theatre. Here's Russia at its best, and theatre-going is not included in the tour. 'They show you only the best!' Quack-quack, quack-quack. They don't, they keep the best from you. You have to find it for yourself.

You see, I met a Director. Another one. And he said I was to present my card at the (I can't possibly spell the name of the theatre) and my seat would be waiting for me. Well, I did that. And after the man at the box office had examined my card and put it away carefully in his pocket, and after I, horrified, had gone through a frantic pantomime of sitting down, watching an invisible but enthralling piece of acting and clapping vigorously, light broke upon him. With great joy he tore off a red ticket, thrust it into my hand and me almost into the arms of an enormous Soviet soldier, crying wildly, 'Frenz—huh? Frenz?' I nodded, we all nodded, and the three of us moved towards the entrance wrapped in a single fraternal embrace. Before I was thrust into the dark auditorium I asked the soldier in French if I should be in time for the first Act. He gaped. The first Act? But no, of course not. They were already at the end of the third. *Mais, comment!* Half-past eight and at the end of the third Act of *Hamlet?*

—*Hamlet?* They stared at me. *Hamlet?* This was a vaudeville—the third act was—— *Milles tonnerres! Gamlet! Vous voulez Gamlet?* Well, Gamlet, if they like it better that way, but one of them—either Hamlet or Gamlet—I must have. Oh, that was two squares further on.

I ran like a hare through Moscow crying 'Gamlet?' and the passers-by pointed me onward as dancers might in a ballet of Hermes. I fell into my seat just before the end of the first Act, but even the little I saw before the lights went up was enough to convince me of two things—that this *Hamlet* was a new one on me and that all tourists, properly to understand Russia, must be taken to a theatre immediately on arrival. Crèches? Fortresses? Nonsense! The life of the country is here.

What a play! It would have broken the professors' hearts, but mine felt like a heart for the

90

first time since I have been in Russia. *Pour arriver à Dieu il faut détourner de Dieu*. Well, they've turned their backs on Hamlet as we know him, but he shone forth more brightly than I've ever seen him. Every possible rule was broken, the text was murderously cut about and great wads of Erasmus and anonymous buffoonery interpolated. The characters, too, were altered. Rosencrantz and Guildenstern became a couple of clowns who were let loose before a drop-curtain every time a scene needed to be changed. But, when you come to think of it, these two *are* rather vaudeville and are easily turned into slapstick comedians. How often have we groaned when some star actor rhetorically hurls at the empty air the question whether it is nobler in the mind—etc, etc, and not even echo makes reply. Not so here. The speech was divided between Hamlet and Horatio. The two students are in the library of the palace, Hamlet turning a globe, Horatio on steps reaching up to a high shelf for a book.

To be or not to be—begins Hamlet.

That is the question, returns Horatio, as one who observes, Boy, you've said it.

And so the speech goes on and for once appears real and the natural comments of very young undergraduates.

Hamlet's advice to the actors and the Play Scene itself was played as a rehearsal in the kitchens of the palace. But since, for the story's sake, the effect of the Play Scene upon the King

91

has to be shown, this was done later in tableau and one had a momentary glimpse of the Court watching, terrified, from the Royal Box.

Ophelia was invited to retire to a nunnery in the most sylvan of woodland scenes, after King, Queen and retinue had galloped past and out of hearing on papier-maché property horses and with cardboard falcons at their wrists. Her great scene came at the end of a Court carouse when she chanted her songs, not mad but dead drunk and supported by a couple of tipsy pages. And she got it over. For once she seemed to me real and unhappy and moving.

A gorgeous lowbrow brawl ended the evening. Fortinbras and his men were the flights of angels that sang the corpses to their rest, and from the way the audience laughed I guessed that a real soldiers' song had been interpolated.

Not *Hamlet*, perhaps, but *Hamlet* enough for me, and I can't help feeling that Shakespeare would have preferred it to highbrow productions that can get a new kick out of Hamlet only by putting him into plus-fours and to those other horrors where *Hamlet* is only a peg to hang scenery on—a Mr. Cochran's Young Gentleman, perhaps.

Of course, I have probably missed the real meaning of *Hamlet* according to Soviet Principles, for I did not hear the lecture by Mr. Bloomberg, but even if I have, what I saw was good enough for me.

But apart from the acting—which was generally

excellent—and the new angle of production—apart, in fact from *Hamlet* itself, the most interesting element of the entertainment was the audience. It was such an audience as all actors dream of and find, as a rule, only in Heaven; an audience that offered itself without reserve, as an instrument might to a musician. And thus there was established between actors and audience that magical current, that invisible but almost tangible stream, in which spectators become participants, and every person in the theatre is acting a specific part in the play. Natural actors, all of them, and one sees very clearly, sitting in a Russian theatre, how it is that the Soviet State has been able to build life up to platform pitch. Add unceasing propaganda and reiterated slogans to a natural aptitude for acting, and you have conditioned your individual for the present régime. Hoardings, megaphones and his own dramatic sense convince him that he is playing a star part in the Bolshevik pageant, that without him the whole fabric of Soviet Russia would crumble to ruins. Oh, it's clever, it's diabolically clever. Lenin discovered that bears dance naturally and Stalin knew well how to put rings in their noses and lead them through the streets. But somewhere, behind all the cunning exploitation, is there not the bear's own desire to be so led? Haven't the people themselves chosen the tyranny that flatters their deepest instincts and relieves them of the necessity of thinking for themselves?

93

The F.P., I find, does NOT think so.

At the Embassy they say this production of
Hamlet is a Sacrilege. One of them actually
Walked Out. Isn't it astonishing the way one so
constantly meets people one thought existed only
in books? These are mostly out of Ouida and un-
believably true. They talk about grouse-shootin',
the B.B.C. and These Dreadful Russians. They
wear striped trousers and morning coats and invisible Union Jacks. One thing only saves me
from rushing out and embracing the first Russian
I meet out of sheer reaction. One thing only—
the cake. Real cake—you never tasted it. Tea
with Milk. Cushions. You don't know how Russia
sharpens the senses. One contracts in one direction but expands magically in others. The sense
of sight remains proportionate, for there is always
something to delight it; but those of sound, smell,
taste and touch have so little work to do that
this enforced rest-cure makes giants of them, sensi-
tive, expectant giants with perceptions never
known before. Infinitesimal things assume enormous significance, the significant fill the sky. . . .
Isn't it a curious paradox that Russia, pledged to
materialism, should have the effect of making us
each a Paracelsus seeing stars in his bread, and
of filling us with immortal longings?. . .

I have discovered that I am being watched—
we all are. Of course, the rest of the party have

been dinning it into my ears ever since we left London that nobody could make a move in Russia without it being known to the whole hierarchy of Chekas. But I laughed at them. It seemed unnecessarily dramatic and such a waste of the Cheka time.

But when I told the hall porter I wanted to ring up T—— in Leningrad and gave him the number, he said, 'Yes, I know. You wish to ring up Comrade T——. It is known that he is your friend. Yes. His telephone is out of order. It is not possible.'

Each day I have asked every visible official to telephone T—— for me (for how can I do it myself when I don't know a word of this ungainly barbaric tongue?) and the reply is always the same. 'We know. He is your friend. It is out of order.'

It is a nuisance, for of course I want to let him know where I've planted the bombs and to ask him what I'm to do with all this gelignite.

Seriously though, there does seem to be something in it. I never go out by myself without being told by a guide where I have been. How is it done? Have I a special bit of the Cheka to myself? And which is he—or she? The woman in the tram yesterday carrying one of those eiderdown bags which (judging from the faint muffled protests one hears coming from within) contain slowly-suffocating babies? Or the man who was knocked down by an ambulance and left on the road to die or recover as he wished? It may be very flattering but it is not good for me for it gives me a false sense of my own importance. It is no good explaining to Intourist that I have friends here and letters of introduction and that anyway even if I hadn't I should want to be alone sometimes. That to them is the worst of evils. A most unhealthy sign. A good Bolshevik never wants to be alone. He is so conditioned that his one desire is to work with the gang, sleep with the gang, and with the gang take his pleasures. Horrible.

But they are getting very cross. And so am I. After all, I bought my ticket (or thought I did) for a tour through Red Russia, and not for a sojourn in the army. Indeed, if this kind of thing goes on, I shall be compelled to *join* the army, for the Soviet soldiers all look happy and well fed. I am told that they get the first pick of whatever good things are going, and are allowed to do exactly what they like. In that case the army is the place for me. It must be a male regiment, however. The female Russian soldier one sees in the streets is a terrifying figure—fee, fi, fo, fum. A single platoon of them could, I am convinced, wipe out the whole of one Western army.

Good-bye—I am going out, alone, to find A—— If you don't hear from me again, my love to all at home. . . .

VI

THE guide has just broken the news. We are not
to go to Nizhny-Novgorod. A lively and dramatic
scene has just been played in the Intourist office.
The party is prepared to swallow the Soviet State
whole, but for an Englishman to purchase a ticket
and then not to be allowed to go to the place in-
dicated upon it is quite another matter. We demanded to know the reason why. We are tired of
doing and dying.

It seems that the boats have broken down.
What, *all* the boats? Impossible. But Intourist
was inexorable and we were compelled ignomini-
ously to retire into a corner and talk over the
situation together, the guides looking on with
contemptuous Mongol faces. But we were not going to allow them to get away with it. If not
Nizhny-Novgorod, then we would insist on some
other equally exciting adventure. A hurried con-
sensus was taken. We were all agreed (though I was
a little dubious about the first diversion) that to
make up for Nizhny we must be taken to a good
Collective Farm and a performance of the Ballet.

Then Intourist retired in a body to another
corner to discuss the ultimatum. Eventually they
accepted it and we were mollified. But there was

something in the eye of Intourist I didn't like. A look that suggests there is a codicil written in invisible ink. They are going to do us down somewhere or I'm a Russian.

We are now all very magnanimous and gentlemanly again and continually assure one another that, after all, Intourist can't help the general breakdown of river shipping, and anyway what's one city more or less when one can see a Collective Farm—tractors, miles of steppes, workers, statistics?

But I am left wondering. Has anybody ever seen Nizhny—any tourist? I doubt it. There was H—— who wrote that appalling sob-stuff book. I remember that he sat on the wharf at Nizhny while waiting for a boat. Perhaps he thought he was seeing the city. And P——, who was actually allowed to land and was driven (being a soft class blackleg) round the outer wall of the motor car factory (which was closed) and then taken back to the ship. He could tell us nothing of Nizhny. *Who* has dwelt upon the holy hill?

I knew it! We have been diddled. We have been to the 'Collective Farm.' It was a cleverly arranged and very comic charade.

Early yesterday morning a superlative motor coach drew up at the hotel. Much elated, the party and an entirely new guide (who apparently thought it would be a waste of time to learn English, for she can hardly speak a word of it) stepped

100

in and were whirled off. We sat in our unaccustomed comfort with scarcely disguised pride and triumph. I thought we looked like a group of Jewish financiers going to a picnic. The coach whizzed pompously through Moscow and we settled down to a long, long drive into the Heart of Russia, dreaming happily of super-seedtimes and harvests. We wondered how many square miles a tractor can plough up in an hour and longed to embrace the (statistical) figures.

After less than half an hour of this, as we were roaring through the outer environs of Moscow, the coach suddenly drew up at a small dilapidated village green. The guide gathered herself together for the plunge into English.

'Let's go.'

Go? Go where? We have only time for a Collective Farm and we have a long day before us.

'Zis Collect Farm,' she said, and waved her hand at a dingy mule grazing on the green and a handful of suburban cottages. With some surprise but innocently convinced that she knew best, we got out. She pointed to the most distant of the cottages, cried 'Zere!' and took her place at the head of the column. We moved off, two and two, behind her. Arrived, we were packed tightly into a little room that appeared to be an office. It was furnished with several shelves, two chairs and a Director. This last began to speak; in fact, he went on speaking for at least an hour, referring from time to time to a large tattered book that in any

101

other country might easily have been taken for a Bible. It occurred to me, for a moment, that we were being treated to a religious service of some secret prohibited sect. But no. The lecture came to an end and the guide began to translate.

'Zis place, she make thirty-three cabbages the year. . . .' We stared at one another with amazement. What had we struck? Thirty-three cabbages!

'Lettuce two sousand. Seven carrots. Nitrates, no it is not. Soil, she is good. Yes. Many workers. Yes. Zey do not eat cabbages. Cabbage for the State.'

A soft ominous murmur was rising from our midst. An idiot could have seen that we had had almost enough—even the School Teachers. The guide was no idiot. For a moment she floundered further, knew suddenly that she was lost, and that her English primer had failed her. Hurriedly, realizing the tenseness of the situation, she broke off——

'Let's go!'

I was sorry for the Director. He looked so sad and disappointed. His beautiful speech, only a hundredth of it translated. Now these English would go away and never know how many tomatoes he had in his glass-house.

We streeled out. At the gate I turned down the road in the direction of the coach.

'Aren't you coming?' said the First Professor.

'I think not. I never cared very much for cabbages.'

'There may be something else,' he said hopelessly.

'I doubt it.' And he went gloomily away.

The driver of the coach unexpectedly turned into a human being when I returned. As I got in he coughed gently, struck his chest and flung out his hand questioningly. I took this to mean that he saw I had a cough and wanted to know was it very bad. I nodded, smiling. With that he dived into some recess under his seat and brought out a grimy bottle and a cup. Beaming he held them up before me.

'Vodka?' he enquired.

I became a mandarin. I could hardly stop nodding and smiling and bowing my appreciation and acceptance. He dusted the cup with his handkerchief, filled it and ceremoniously handed it to me. You know the taste of poteen. Well, it isn't a bit like that. Yet more like it than any other drink. Liquid fire. I drank the lot and then the driver had his share and smuggled the bottle away again. We sat there gleaming at each other, utterly happy, the horizon gradually becoming blurred, the trees doubling themselves and dancing, and somehow there seemed to be four mules instead of one on the green, moving rather unevenly in a row. The cottages were going up and down the sky like swings at a fair. It was lovely!

Suddenly I heard a little squeak of a voice beside the coach. I looked out. About six little boys (or it may have been one little boy repeated several times, a recurring decimal on legs—vodka is very potent) were cheeping at me. '*Tovarish, tovarish, tovarish.*' I dived into my bag. Yes—there was the cake of chocolate the First Professor had bought for me yesterday. I broke it into very small pieces, and the creatures ate out of my hand like birds. Presently a huge loutish youth came sauntering out of a cottage. When he saw what was going on he scattered the children with one great sweep of his arm and began a lengthy speech to them. I guessed, from the occasional contemptuous glance he threw in my direction, that he was reminding them of the tenets of their religion. To take meat (or chocolate, which was worse) from the hands of the capitalist, shame upon them! Hadn't they, citizens of the Soviet State, more pride? What would become of them in the future? Lenin alone knew.

Then he turned away, well pleased with his peroration. Immediately his back was turned, the swarming began again. And again the scattering. Until it became a game. Each time the children swarmed they seemed to have increased in number and I don't think this was entirely due to the vodka. I was feeding a whole regiment of Octobrists (young Bolsheviki) by the time the rest of the party returned.

'It's only a nursery garden,' said the First Professor, who was a little ahead of the others.

'It's only a nursery garden, in a beautiful golden —No, no, Professor, I don't mean that. Don't listen to me. I'm drunk. Vodka!' His eyes gleamed.

'Where did you get it?' A gesture was enough to convince the driver that the F.P. was my particular friend and he dived and came up holding the treasure in his hand.

The sight of the First Professor drinking vodka out of a bottle is one that will remain with me for ever. But the stern glance with which he impaled me forbade any comment.

On the way home he told me between roars of vodkanian laughter that they had seen yet another crèche, a collection of hot-houses and several rows of young beetroot. From the way he spoke I gathered he was tired of babies and didn't any more care much for vegetables.

It was no good storming at Intourist. They insisted, with the lie clear on their faces, that we *had* seen a Collective Farm. When we told them, with a few apt adjectives, that we'd done nothing of the sort, their manner became full of uplift, and we were allowed to infer that their study of the English language had not included a course in anathema and that they, personally, were glad of this fact. . . .

An awful contretemps has occurred. It happened last night at the Ballet. Oh yes, we've been to the Ballet all right. I was disappointed that it was not one of the more modern performances. *Lac des*

Cygnes is sufficiently antiquated to make one think one is still living under the Tsarist régime. Technically the dancing was superb. The least of it was better than anything we can do in the West. The addition of a 'ski' or a 'pow' to an English name cannot add Russian oil and wine to English blood. I should have preferred, however, to have seen a ballet where the classical technique, released from the set mould of tradition, is expanded so as to include new forms and interpretations, instead of being, as it was in the *Lac*, a splendid *tour de force*.

Again, as at *Hamlet*, the audience was the perfect audience. One felt that nameless magical juice flowing through one's self, too, and had that rare sense of harmony that comes when a great number of people are equally sharing in delight. In the theatre I felt entirely at one with the Russians, probably because the theatre is the only place where they become a collection of liberated human beings instead of functioning as members of groups, cells and soviets. Thus the affair of the Third Professor and the Poultry Farmer was all the more distressing.

The three Professors, the Poultry Farmer, two School Teachers and myself shared a *loge* with two or three Russians. One of these turned out, on closer acquaintance, achieved by means of halting French phrases, to be the brother-in-law of M——, the violinist. He was inordinately proud of the relationship so I did not tell him that we think the violinist rather a bad one. He told me the names of all the dancers and hissed the story of the ballet into my ear at intervals. The audience, after the performance of a splendid *pas seul*, rose to its feet waving its programmes and shouting.

Imagine my horror then when among all this babble of praise I heard the word 'Liar!' just behind me. I turned. The Third Professor and the Poultry Farmer were taking the opportunity, under cover of the noise, to speak their minds. (They have always hated each other and now their antagonism has broken bounds.) The lights went up and the audience dropped exhausted into its seats. But the T.P. and the P.F. had tasted blood and wanted a kill. They continued their argument, hurling discourteous epithets at each other with the most villainous intent, but all the time preserving fixed smiles upon their faces for the benefit of the Russians, who must not be allowed to witness an Englishman's loss of composure. A deaf-and-dumb Hottentot would have found it difficult not to realize what was happening and the Russians were naturally very astonished.

The T.P. turned to me, smiling sicklily. 'Did you or did you not hear him call me a——?'

'What does he say?' hissed the Brother-in-Law in my ear.

What must I answer? If I say I did hear it, I range myself against the P.F. If I say I didn't, the Third Professor will think I'm holding the Land of Hope and Glory episode up against him.

107

'Tell me what he says!' The Brother-in-Law is getting impatient.

'Hush! They are discussing the dancing. The English are very serious about dancing, they get excited at a *pas-bas*, a *plié* inflames them, and an *entrechat*——'

The Brother-in-Law doesn't look as if he believed me.

It is all very difficult. Eventually a sort of truce is patched up and by the time the interval is over each is sitting with his back to the other staring furiously into space. But the harmony of the evening is broken. All through the succeeding Acts I am conscious of that ominous undercurrent of recrimination behind me.

'If I ever again hear you . . . call me . . . knock your head . . . shouldn't wonder . . . you're a spy . . . pay of Russia . . . You say that again. . . . Go on, say it—you. . . .'

'*Incroyable!*' mutters the Brother-in-Law, half to himself and half to me. '*Incroyable!*'

The Poultry Farmer and the Third Professor walked home from the ballet on opposite sides of the street. They are still in a state of war, and I, the unwitting and unwilling participant, spend my time carrying white flags and doves from one to the other.

Once all this would have amused me, but I am rather weary of antagonisms. The English are wound up to the limit, in order to retain within themselves the mood of earnest appreciation, the

108

Russians tight and set in their Soviet mould. No wonder there are explosions. Will life ever flow again? Gorse shining from the dark hollow of a hill, cattle knee-deep in green; the bright fields of Ireland, with their daily act of transubstantiation, grass becoming flesh—do these really exist outside my memory? Oh dear . . .

Today, walking through the Red Square, I saw a worker wheeling a barrow piled high with bronze busts of Lenin and Stalin. The soldiers on guard at the Kremlin Gate, seeing the sacred (mass-produced) load, sprang to attention and saluted smartly. I was shocked to see that the wheeler of the barrow was so far lost to the solemnity of the occasion that he was still wearing his hat.

VII

VII

I HAVE touched the high peak of the tour. I have been to tea with a Member of the Communist Party. When M—— told me that I simply must meet A—— I took it calmly enough. I didn't know then what a distinguished person he was. My dear, he has two rooms *and* a kitchen!

I arrived, after having held up before half Moscow my little piece of paper with A——'s address printed on it in block capitals, expecting to find the usual one-room apartment crowded with babies, grandfathers, sisters and cousins and aunts. Instead, I found A—— and his wife alone. It seemed unnatural, somehow.

But he deserves it. Do you know that he is seven Directors? He is also a selection of Advisory Committees, Secretary to a Writer's Club and a successful playwright. He intends shortly to begin translating English and American books into Russian, and his first remark to me was an injunction to send him the complete works of Gertrude Stein for this purpose when I got back to England.

At first our conversation was very hygienic, swept with a smart new broom. I could see he was courteously restraining his contempt for most of our Western customs and I was treading carefully so as not to be brought up against a controversial subject. Besides, I was enchanted with the little colored biscuits and the samovar and the warmth, and I did not want to have to leave all these before I was disenchanted.

Then suddenly he broke down the whole careful shelter that together we had built.

'You are for the Soviet State—yes?'

I hesitated.

'Ah-h-h!' His blue eyes gleamed. He saw a possible convert. And I found myself embarked upon the stormiest of seas. He and his wife. The two of them—it wasn't fair.

He passed triumphantly from point to point, demonstrating very clearly the absurdity of mentioning any civilization in the same breath with the Soviet State. From Workers we went to Shock Brigades, from Shock Brigades to Communist cells, from these to Komsomols and then on to the Co-operatives—you have no idea of the number of different grades of workers there are in proletarian Russia!

His eyes had the tranced expression I have come to know so well, but in a greater degree than the ordinary Russian because, of course, he is a member of the Party. And while he spoke I kept trying to see behind that façade the real person. Could it be that Soviet Principles were not merely printed upon him but engraved? It was difficult to believe this—he was so intelligent, so quickly fired to further flights by my own chance words.

114

He took a breath and went on.

'Now the authors and artists—let us look at them.' And we looked at them. First in their beautiful apartments in the House of Writers and the House of Artists. Each man had a room, a bed, a chair and a table: was paid by the State and assured that he would never be hungry any more.

'But surely poverty, and hunger, within limits, of course, have often been——' He was at the end of my thought before I had finished giving it shape.

'The artist's necessary friction? Ah, but all that is over. Now that he is kept by the State his friction will come from thought fretting upon thought——'

I forbore to tell him it would probably come from living in a House of Writers, despite the bed, chair, table, etc. Not that I would have had the chance, for he had already gone on to another Soviet Principle—one that, in essence, saves the artist the necessity of thinking out his own themes.

Roughly, there appear to be three themes for the artist in Soviet Russia—the Fall of Tsardom, the Revolution, and the Emergence of the new (Bolshevik) man. As he enumerated these and airily blew away everything that occurred in history before the famous Fall, my conviction that this Soviet State has an intimate relation to early (even present-day) Christianity was intensified. They both share the same *nouveau riche* idea that before the emergence of their own particular ava-

115

tar—Lenin or Jesus—chaos lay dark upon the
world. Both proclaim the doctrine of Work the
Only Good, and elevate the Producer to the
status of deity. Both practice mariolatry—bring
forth, bring forth, bring forth! And the reward?
More bringing forth. Do you remember last year's
papal edict? The sense was— 'Rich, be generous!
Poor, be patient, there are other rewards!' Does
not the latter half of this humane (*sic*) command
read rather like a present-day Soviet slogan? *What*
other rewards? For the poor Christians a future
Heaven, for the poor Bolsheviki a future Super-
state. The world is full of rewards but the genera-
tions die without being allowed to know it. Lenin,
indeed, was the first man to tell them and to de-
clare himself for Paradise Here and Now. But he
did not live long enough. His name flickers in and
out everywhere in Russia like an elusive star; but
his splendid immediacy, his undeviating pursuit
of reality, his preoccupation with the everlasting
Now—where are these? What renegade doctrine
has eclipsed them?

The 'new' religion, of course!

A——, assisted occasionally by his wife, was
climbing flight after flight of rhetoric. And as
they talked I had the feeling that they, like all
the Russians I have met, were talking against
time, unconsciously blowing the great bubble of
their belief to its inevitable breaking point, headlong rushing towards disintegration, chaos and
life.

I tried to put this feeling into words.

A——, however, ploughed ecstatically through my murmurings, warming to his peroration.

'The Sickle and the Hammer, Work for All, the Soul of every Russian——'

'I thought,' I suggested meekly, 'that such an exclusively personal and individual possession as a soul——'

But there was no room for me upon his visionary heights.

How it came about I don't know, but in a chance and soft aside to his wife I happened to mention the word lemons.

Immediately A—— came down with a bang.

'Lemons? Did you say lemons?'

And his face completely changed. Gone was the tranced gleam, the fanatical enthusiasm. He looked human and very beautiful with the lines of his face suddenly softened and mobile and joyous.

'You said lemons. Have you lemons?' I nodded. And the gigantic creature leapt across the room and shook me by the shoulders with a sort of loving anger.

'And you did not tell me. I *thought* you were not being quite natural. I have been talking and talking all the time and *you* have been keeping the secret. Come. We will go in my motor-car. Not one more minute. Take the sugar biscuits. All of them. Yes, all. Not one more minute. My hat, Natasha! I go for the lemons.'

How beautiful people are when they laugh like that. O fragile bubble of theories, broken by a little fruit with a rough yellow rind! How little sun it needs to melt a frozen river.

When he stood in the hall of the hotel with eight lemons clasped to his breast A———, freed from his Communist mould, was blushing and suffused and shy. He did not know what to say, he could only babble idiocies among which I distinguished certain phrases.

He would not forget. Never, never. He had always thought the Irish race the most charming, the most imaginative, the most understanding—and wouldn't it be better if he put them in his hat? They would be safer there.

But he did not look at me as he spoke; he was really addressing the lemons. The Prodigal Son himself did not get a better welcome.

I turned from watching him drive away, to find the hall-porter mutely and imploringly gazing at me. I understood. Fixing him sternly with my eye I said: 'I want to telephone to Leningrad. If I get the number———' He flew to the telephone box like a bird.

Half an hour later I was summoned to speak to T———. He had been expecting to hear from me. Why the delay? They said his telephone was out of order. The devil they did—of course it wasn't.

Well, the hall-porter has his lemon. There will be six happy homes to-night. For I couldn't refuse those other mute appeals in the office of the

118

hotel. There were only six lemons left, so I threw them in the air among them and they scrambled for the fruit like children at a party. Then suddenly they all went mad and began throwing the lemons backwards and forwards to each other, crying and laughing and shouting.

Oh—it wasn't the lemons, much as they wanted them. Something stretched too tensely had suddenly snapped, and warmth, friendliness, life—call it what you like—was flowing among us.

One hit the First Professor on the nose as the rest of the party came in from a visit to the University (I mean the House of Learning). He picked it up and threw it, and somebody else threw it again until we were all half-backs and centres and forwards in some fantastic cup-final of lemons.

We are free, all of us. Russians and tourists, we are free for a moment of time, winged and untrammelled beneath the changing arcs of yellow fruit.

O Captain, my Captain, our fearful trip is done. Or very nearly. We are waiting at the Douane at Leningrad for the word to go aboard. Winds are blowing from the Pole Star; behind us the cold better land keeps its secrets; before us lies the cold companionable sea. Everybody, except myself, tries to hide his satisfaction that the Russian tour is well and truly over. But I see it glimmering through their solemnity, and their steps are light and jaunty.

'Well—it has all been very interesting—very interesting,' says the First Professor ponderously.

Chorus of 'Verys!'

'I think,' I say suggestively, 'I shall come again next year.'

Every man fish of them rises to the bait.

'What—YOU!'

'Well, one never knows. It may be quite different then.'

Hearty, derisive laughter, suggesting that they are sure—indeed, that they *hope* it will not be different.

But in spite of so much concerted hope and sureness it may be. Think of A——'s changed and softened face, his armor gone in a moment. Think of the battle of lemons. It may be. Canst thou bind the sweet influence of the Pleiades? Or loose the bands upon Orion?

We are nearly home. Whoever called the North Sea a waste? It is the loveliest and kindest of seas.

We are all dazed and weary with sorting out our impressions. I notice a curious tendency—everybody seems anxious to go off into a corner by himself. Can they have so soon forgotten that their duty is to merge, simply to merge? Lonely and withdrawn, what are they thinking there in their chosen corners? Hush, do not disturb them. They are asleep.

To-day I had news for the First Professor and found him reading avidly a largish book with a brown-paper cover. He closed it hurriedly as I appeared.

'Professor, I have just discovered that twenty-two times round the deck is half a mile, that we took on fourteen loaves of bread, six cauliflowers and a bag of onions at Kiel, that the average rate of pay for Soviet seamen is——'

'Will you *never* be serious?' said the First Professor, sighing heavily.

At that moment the ship gave a gentle little lurch and as the Professor swung with the roll his book fell open. I could not help seeing the title. It read—*Three-Gun Finnigan*. By Elliott Putnam Vine. Author of *Murder by Moonlight*.

I looked at the First Professor.

The First Professor looked at me.

It was a long, steady look of complete understanding. . . .

P. L. TRAVERS

LATE last fall, with the publication of an extraordinary book called MARY POPPINS, a new name was added to that highly select group of authors of books which are delightful both to children and adults, the group which includes Lewis Carroll and A. A. Milne. The author of this book about the Banks children and their incredible governess was P. L. Travers.

She is a young Irish woman who lives in a thirteenth century cottage in Sussex in the summer and in a not-so-old and not-at-all English cottage in the south of France in the winter.

MARY POPPINS, she says, is probably made up of all the Nannies she played in as a child in the British Isle where she was born. More

carrie

Check Out More Titles From HardPress Classics Series In this collection we are offering thousands of classic and hard to find books. This series spans a vast array of subjects – so you are bound to find something of interest to enjoy reading and learning about.

Subjects:
Architecture
Art
Biography & Autobiography
Body, Mind &Spirit
Children & Young Adult
Dramas
Education
Fiction
History
Language Arts & Disciplines
Law
Literary Collections
Music
Poetry
Psychology
Science
…and many more.

Visit us at www.hardpress.net

SD - #0142 - 230123 - C0 - 229/152/8 - PB - 9780461115673 - Gloss Lamination